in GOD'S PRESENCE

in GOD'S PRESENCE

Theological Reflections on Prayer

By
Marjorie Hewitt Suchocki

CHALICE
PRESS

ST. LOUIS, MISSOURI

Biblical quotations, unless otherwise noted, are from the *New Revised Standard Version Bible,* copyright 1989, Division of Christian Education of the National Council of the Churches of Christ in the USA. Used by permission.

Art direction: Lynne Condellone
Cover design and photo: Arista Graphics

Visit Chalice Press on the World Wide Web at
www.chalicepress.com

10 9 8 7   04 05 06 07

Library of Congress Cataloging–in–Publication Data

Suchocki, Marjorie.
    In God's presence : theological reflections on prayer / Marjorie
        Hewitt Suchocki.
            p. cm.
        ISBN 0–8272–1615–7
        1. Prayer—Christianity.   I. Title.
    BV215.S83   1996
    248.3'2—dc20   96-14006
                                                        CIP

Printed in the United States of America

for

JOAN SUCHOCKI LUCAS

Contents

Acknowledgments

For many years I have wanted to write this book, expressing my own personal theological reflections on the great gift of prayer. I wanted it to be a book for Christians like myself who found themselves wondering, even while maintaining a life of prayer, "how it works." Merely pondering this question, however, does not seem to be enough. There is an urge to share one's reflections, and to ask: "Does it seem like this to you, too?"

I am grateful to my daughter, Joan Lucas (to whom this book is lovingly dedicated) for her many helpful suggestions. If my goal of writing in laity-friendly language is achieved, it is largely due to her. My neighbor and colleague, Kathy Black, also cast her critical and liturgically sophisticated eyes over the manuscript. And my good friends and colleagues in Germany, Michael and Ulrike Welker, spent a sunny morning in August on their terrace discussing the book with me, tossing titles back and forth until they helped me to decide that this book really should be "In God's Presence"—because that's what the book is about.

CHAPTER ONE

The Question of Prayer

Sometimes I make appointments with God. God, being the God of all time and eternity, presumably has no constraints on time, but we creatures often do. And when matters of sufficient urgency press upon me that require more than ordinary work in prayer, I find it helpful to suggest something like a 2:00 a.m. session, when interruptions are not apt to occur. Such appointments seem only sensible—and I am deeply grateful for such times. But it occurs to me upon occasion that it is certainly an odd thing to be able to talk with the God of the universe, whether at 2:00 a.m. or any other time.

Have you never thought it peculiar, this matter called prayer? Have you not also wondered from time to time how such an amazing thing can be? Sometimes amazement can turn to questioning the reality of this thing called prayer. How could God pay attention to such insignificant creatures as ourselves? On another front, what if prayer is simply a way of talking things over with oneself? How do we *know* that prayer is communication with God? Put another way, how do we know that it's God that we know when we think that we know God?

The very asking of such questions leads to one of the oldest definitions of Christian theology: faith seeking understanding. To probe the questions is to trust God in the very probing, knowing that God can handle all the questions we can devise. Questions can be a way of drawing us into deeper realms of faith, taking us from belief in our beliefs to belief in the God who is more than our beliefs can express. But if God is more than we can express, then there is freedom to think far and wide, critically exploring how we think and how we might think about the issues of faith. Faith seeks understanding.

What, then, about the question of prayer in relation to our own insignificance in the universe? Perhaps in earlier times prayer did not raise such a question. Then Christians saw Earth as the center of a universe. Then, as now, God was understood to be the God of the universe and not simply the God of this earth. Then, as now, the heavens and the earth were considered mysterious beyond comprehension. "Where were you when I laid the foundations of the earth?" is God's answer to the pretentiousness of Job. But earth was the focal point, and humanity was the culmination of all God's creation. Prayer in such a universe was natural, for if the whole universe culminates in humanity, then surely it is not peculiar that humanity is bidden to be in communion with the creator.

Today we no longer live in a human-centered universe. Earth is but one planet in one solar system in one galaxy. We are dwarfed by the vastness of the universe beyond ourselves, and we no longer have the simple confidence that it was all created so that we ourselves might exist. Stars spin in distant space, and explode, perhaps becoming condensed gravity fields so dense that not even light escapes their force, perhaps drawing other stars into each darkened vortex. Stars beyond number form myriad galaxies, vast spirals of dancing light. Comets, asteroids, nebulae, suns, moons, planets, all whirl in what seems to be an infinite creation of expanding space; how are we to consider ourselves a privileged center in a universe now seen to be so complex that it no longer has a center? And how and where is God in all this awesome space? Is God outside it? Inside it? Nowhere? Everywhere? Is the God of Genesis who creates a universe culminating in human history the same God if construed as God of this very different creation? Do we simply expand the God of biblical texts? Is prayer still applicable to a God of the universe of which we are such an infinitesimal part?

If we turn our eyes to the smaller scale of human history, do we still understand that the God of the galaxies takes an interest in our histories? Once we thought the Earth was a stage set for the drama of ourselves; now we know that millennia of actors played this stage before us, and perhaps millennia of actors will succeed us. In the short time of our human existence we have not only taken over the stage, but we seem to be doing our best to destroy the sets. Can we really believe that creatures such as our sorry selves in the littleness of our histories are invited by the creator of the universe to pray?

If the insignificance of human history is not itself seen to be such a challenge to prayer, then what of the multiple modes of human history? Once we thought that a single people was chosen by God from out of all the rest for singular communion; we Christians then saw ourselves as superseding God's original choice, but in either case, the perception was that God spoke with some, but not with all. However, just as Earth is no longer a privileged center in the universe, neither is one history a privileged center among histories. All peoples pray. What does it do to our understanding of prayer when it ceases to be the prerogative of a single religious history?

These are some of the questions that grow from our awareness of our insignificance in the universe and within Earth's history. It can seem so improbable, given our reduced estimate of our importance, that we should have a direct line of communication to the power that brings the universe into existence. As we move away from our own centrality and discover a universe so enormous and complex, then the image of God bringing a universe into existence for the sole purpose of making us humans becomes a bit tenuous.

But notice the assumptions hidden in these questions. One is that all things cannot be equally important to God, and since we are relatively insignificant in the great scheme of things, we must be beyond the divine care. Another is that there is a fundamental separation between God and that which God creates, so that God is in no way necessarily in continuous relation with creation. But perhaps God creates not as a power over an inert matter molded into form, with a single purpose, but as a power *with* all matter, present to it, pervading it with presence, with multiple purposes.

Think of water as a different metaphor for God. Water rushes to fill all the nooks and crannies available to it; water swirls around every stone, sweeps into every crevice, touches all things in its path—and changes all things in its path. The changes are subtle, often slow, and happen through a continuous interaction with the water that affects both the water and that which the water touches. Particles of sand and sediment change the color of the water, and the water's action changes the stone, and the land, and the life that can be supported. The water doesn't exert its power by being "single-minded" over and above these things, but simply by being pervasively present to and with all things. It does not evoke the "command" of power over its creation; it is more like a "persuasive" power with and around its creation. Its power is a power of presence.

What if God is like that? Could we not imagine a God pervasively present throughout all the universe, filling all its vast and small spaces, its greatest galaxies and its tiniest motes of stardust? If God's power works through presence, and if God's presence is an "omnipresence," then one could say both that there is no center to the universe and that everything in the universe is center to all else. There is no center, for all things are "equidistant" from God, and the centeredness of God is unbounded. But, paradoxically, we can say that all things are center, for if all things are in the presence of God, then it is God who centers them. The Earth, then, is indeed privileged, and we do have a privileged history—but so is every space and every history privileged, for all are presenced and centered by God. One could as easily say that some small planet in the Andromeda Galaxy is a focus of God's gracious work as to say that Earth is a focus of God's gracious work. For if God is omnipresent, centering all things, then God is like the rushing water of the universe, filling all spaces, honoring all spaces, centering all spaces through the specialness of divine presence. Prayer in such a universe makes eminent sense—for God is always present. And perhaps this divine presence invites us into communion.

But the second question challenging prayer still remains—not the question of our insignificance, but the question of the limits of our knowledge. How do we know that it's God that we know when we think that we know God? When we pray, do we *really* talk to God, or are we indulging instead in simple meditative communion with ourselves?

There was a time when we all thought that our knowledge of all things—including God—was much simpler than now appears. We thought our knowledge was a direct image of the things we knew in our world. Through our senses we received images of things, and from these images we developed knowledge. Knowledge was like a mirror of the world, duplicating physical reality with thought reality.

Even though our ideas of God were not developed out of sense perceptions, we nonetheless assumed that knowledge of God, like knowledge of the world, reflected God accurately. There was always the qualification, of course, that it is impossible to know the fullness of God—but what we *could* know of God was reliable. Some of this knowledge was mediated by our senses, for it was considered possible to read something about the creator from the works of creation. But the basic knowledge of God came not through the sense but through God's self-revelation, recorded as Scripture by our ancestors in the faith. The knowledge of the world gained through our senses was called natural knowledge, while the knowledge of God gained through revelation was called supernatural knowledge. Like natural knowledge, supernatural knowledge conferred a direct reflection of that which was known. We considered such knowledge spiritual and derived from God. Therefore, it was even more sure than natural knowledge, which related to the inferior material world. And so we confidently prayed to the God we so confidently knew.

But our contemporary understanding of knowledge takes us away from the simpler world of natural and supernatural knowledge. In doing so, it tends to uproot us from that simpler interpretation of the God to whom we pray. Now we know that *what* we know is determined as much by our human psychic and sensory structures as it is by that which we say we know.

My first introduction to the complexities of knowledge came some years ago when I happened upon a photograph of an insect's eye. Unlike ours, the insect's eye was composed of many facets, which affected the way the insect could see. An artist had then constructed an image of a tree as it would look from the insect's point of view; how different it was from the tree that I perceived! The question naturally occurred: which of us saw the tree correctly? If that insect had consciousness, would not that insect insist just as assuredly as I that the "real" tree looked thus and so? How could I be so sure that my knowledge of the tree corresponded to the "real" tree, whereas the insect's did not? For we both knew the tree through our seeing; one seeing could not be more privileged than the other, since they both depended upon the particular structure of the eye as well as upon the structure of that which was seen. What we know is the way an object is given to our senses, not the object as it exists apart from our senses. Our knowing, then, is a combination of the givenness of that which we sense, the structures imposed by our senses, and the further structures imposed by our minds.

These further structures are personal as well as physiological. We bring a cumulative history to our knowing that shapes how and what we can know. How we have been loved, how we have been educated, how and where we have been reared, all affect the interpretations that we impose on the information we receive. Our histories give us the emotional and valuational elements of knowledge, so that even in so simple a knowledge as that of a tree, what we know is more than what the senses perceive.

When I was a child, the oak tree outside my window had a particular branch that to my childish eyes was shaped like a lady; many a nighttime going-to-sleep moment was spent looking at my "lady." For me, the oak trees have never lost their mystical, "lady" aura. Now when I see an oak tree, I see the tree, but also, even so many years later, feel my memories of what that kind of tree meant to me as a child. I "know" oak trees in a way peculiarly shaped by my history! I "see" the tree with my eyes *and* with my memories, as well as with all the knowledge about trees in general and oak trees in particular that I have accrued along the way. My knowledge of any oak tree is a complex combination of things shared with others and things private to myself.

So, then, knowledge is actually a very complex thing reflecting not simply the thing we say that we know but our sensory responses, our mental processes, our emotions, and our personal and cultural histories. We know a mixture of ourselves and the other! Today we know far better than in former times how much our own interpretive capacities are involved in all our knowing. And if this affects our knowing of things like trees, does it not affect even more radically our knowing of God, who is not given to our senses at all?

The issue is complicated because knowledge gained through our senses is grounded to some degree in that which we see, hear, touch, smell, or taste. That is, while whatever we are knowing can be interpreted in a number of ways, those ways are limited by the stubborn facticity of that which we say we know. While a tree may look one way to a human and another to the insect, the tree itself lays down the parameters within which it may be interpreted. A living tree cannot be construed accurately as if it were a cloud or a person, even though sometimes its shape might suggest such things to us. The tree itself will neither rain upon the earth nor tuck us into bed at night, no matter how much we may think that the tree is something like a cloud or a person. It "insists" upon its treeness, regardless of whoever or whatever is doing the perceiving and knowing! What we as humans know about trees can be tested through our direct interactions with the tree, and through common knowledge about trees that we learn from and share with others in the human community.

But testing what we call our knowledge of something not given through sensory perception at all is a more difficult matter. What constrains our interpretations, keeping them within the limits of that reality we say we know? Given the complexity of knowledge, and the contribution of our own psychic histories to those things we "know," how do we know that we are in contact with God rather than just talking to ourselves? How do we know that it's God that we know when we think that we know God? The very complexity of knowing can challenge what we say we know, and erode our confidence in prayer.

But if God's power is presence, think of the difference this makes to the knowing of God. God's presence, like water, pervades the nooks and crannies of existence—what is the boundary of water? the boundary of God? A stone marks the edge of the water and its own existence; what marks the edge between our own and God's existence? Where does our existence begin and end?—for surely we neither start nor stop with our skin. Would it be so strange to consider that the omnipresent God pervades us without at all displacing us? After all, we know quite well that we coexist with many things without this shared space diminishing or displacing our own personhood. Energy waves regularly go through us. And we know that even within us there is a host of life forms such as bacteria. But this co-occupation of space does not make us less ourselves. Why can't the higher life form that is God also co-occupy us, flowing through and around and in us, even while remaining God, and while we remain ourselves? What if such a God affects us at the deepest levels of our being— our most subconscious psyches—as well as at our "edges" in our interaction with the rest of the world? A God of pervasive presence would be no stranger to our psyches; perhaps our access to this God is in and through this deeper intimacy of ourselves in and through prayer. Perhaps, given the pervasiveness of God, we do not *need* sensory perception for the knowledge of God.

What saves us from our rampant imaginations, distinguishing this relational knowing from wishful and wistful delusions? To return to my metaphor of water, if stones and fish could "know," then a stone would know water in one way, and a fish might know water in yet another, for the water interacts with each according to its kind, even while remaining water. Would not a God of presence interact with us in ways adapted to our physiological, psychological, and sociological realities? God knows how we know! And perhaps God, while immaterial, nonetheless radiates an energy that can be interpreted in only so many ways by us humans.

And yet there is also an external check on our knowledge. God is present not simply to us as individuals, but to us as communities. We can check the adequacy of our own knowing through the witness of others—and here the texts and the traditions as well as our contemporary communities play a formative role. We usually interpret God through the texts and traditions we have received from our community, and we shape our own private religious experience by what we have learned publicly. A living community of faith guides our own interpretation of our subjective experience of God.

The caveat, of course, is the living nature of the community and its traditions. A tradition is built up through its continual transformation. For example, those Christians who have been dominantly important in the formation of Western Christianity are persons such as Augustine, Gregory the Great, Anselm, Thomas Aquinas, Martin Luther, John Calvin, Thomas Hooker, Anne

Hutchinson, John Wesley, Alexander Campbell, Aimee Semple McPherson, and a host of others. Some of these people are common in the heritage of all Western Christians; others are important to particular denominations. The point is that none of these persons simply repeated what was said before. Indeed, we study such persons precisely because they thought *differently* from those who went before! Each added to the tradition by contributing to its transformation.

Tradition is like the crest of a wave always pushing beyond itself. Faithfulness to a tradition is not gained through treading water in repetition of some aspect of the past, but through swimming with the crest into fresh interpretations of God's gracious presence with us. The tradition is a living, fluid thing. Thus to use the texts and the tradition as a formative matrix for our knowledge of God is not to find an ironclad rule that determines what we can think. Rather, it is to find commonalities that not only shape how we think about the God we experience, but that also invite the questions born of faith. We know God through God's presence to us, and we interpret this presence through categories given to us through our communities of faith. But the personalization of these categories may in fact be part of their transformation in the ongoing process of a living tradition. Thus there is necessarily a certain openness in what we dare to call our knowledge of God. It is fluid—perhaps like God's own self.

The complexity of these ways of knowing God cautions us to value deeply the ancient Christian virtue of humility. In the old ways of supernatural versus natural knowledge, we could arrogantly claim that the way *we* knew God was the way *everyone* should know God. Today we know that our knowledge of God reflects our personal and cultural histories as much if not more than it does God's own self. We know God in the humility of knowing that others, too, whether inside or outside our own tradition, also have valid ways of knowing God. If God is pervasively present, then God works in and through many communities, each of which then "sees" God through the lens of its own tradition. One set of lenses fitted to one people does not invalidate the lenses that fit another! In the words of the apostle Paul, "now we see in a mirror, dimly," and "now I know only in part." We do not and cannot yet know God in God's fullness.

But the partial and relative nature of our knowledge does not invalidate our knowing. To the contrary, all knowledge that matters is partial and relative: what we look for is a sufficient knowledge. Absolute knowledge is not and never has been required for faith, and the former supposition that we had such knowledge led to hatred and destruction toward those whose knowledge differed from our own. To be content with a sufficient rather than absolute knowledge is to accept that the God of presence is made adequately known to us even within the limitations of our knowing. God is known in the "breaking of the bread" that is ourselves within our own communities. We dare to say that it's God that we know, mixed in with ourselves in a way that is blessed.

A God of presence renders suspect any so-called objective knowledge of God, and calls instead for an intersubjective knowledge of God. Such a knowledge will never be universal—it is too mingled with ourselves for that. And so it should be: It is the way of God's working, and it can yield an adequate knowledge for our living. We can test its contribution to the depth and richness of human community; we can test its effectiveness in our own lives; we can test its truth for our spirits through prayer. For a God of presence, known subjectively and intersubjectively in and through ourselves, our texts, our traditions, and our communities, is a God who invites communion. How do we know that it's God that we know when we think that we know God? The answer is finally the simple one that pervades the trajectory of our tradition: by faith, seeking understanding. And so we pray—in God's presence.

CHAPTER TWO

Images of God

We often think of God as knowing not only the past, but the future, exactly as it will happen, long before it does. And this God who knows us as we are and as we will be also is all-powerful, such that there are no constraints beyond God's own self to inhibit God's actions. What God wills, God can do. Further, we have considered that what God wills, God has willed from all eternity. But if this is the case, what sense does it make to ask things of God in prayer? Has God not already either willed or not willed the actions about which we pray?

Sometimes the images we use of God in prayer reflect this kind of dilemma in paradoxical ways. We think of a God who knows all things, can do all things, and needs nothing, whereas the petitioner is ignorant, impotent, and needy. But strangely enough, our habits of prayer can reverse the images, making us the all-powerful ones and God our servant. For example, we sometimes seem to imagine God as equivalent to the great genie in Aladdin's bottle, with prayer as the magic rubbing that draws the genie forth to do our bidding. Such imaging surely attributes great power to God, much more than we ourselves possess, and so apparently the image intends honor to God. However, the image shifts the control of power to the one who rubs the bottle. Similarly, we can hold an attitude toward God and prayer that seemingly casts us in the role of dictating our memo for the day to our divine secretary, who is then to translate the memo from words to actions. While we assume that God-as-secretary, like God-as-genie, has the power to do the work for which we pray, the control of that power has shifted to the one who prays. In both cases, we use prayer to inform God of the condition, needs, and hopes of the world and ourselves. Receiving the information, God is then to act. To state the role of prayer in such a way reveals the absurdity of the assumptions hidden within such images of prayer. That we use such images, even implicitly, follows from the conundrum of the role of prayer given an all-powerful and all-knowing God.

Another image answering the question of why we pray to a God who is all-powerful and all-knowing casts God in the role of a divine egotist. "God likes to be asked," said a woman of deep faith when she explained why prayer was necessary. All power is attributed to God, but it is as if the divine ego needs to be stroked in a particularly pleasing way for God to respond to the petitioner's request. One must pay the appropriate compliments to God, proving in the process that one is astute enough to note these divine qualities. If we but use the correct formula, the right adjectives, then God will be pleased and will answer us.

A similar image of God is that of a king holding audience, who might grant the petitioner a boon. Here it is as if the king knows thoroughly the situation of the petitioner, but refrains from acting until properly asked. Power here is shifted from petitioner to king, but if the king knows the need, is the king not less than gracious to withhold help until the request is duly given? Perhaps one could argue that the true need of the petitioner is to acknowledge the source of her or his help, and thus the king does well to wait for the petition. The child will not be cured, the peace will not be restored, the food will not be given, until the commoner realizes that health, peace, and plenty belong to the king alone. The king is under no obligation to share this health, peace, and plenty—but if properly acknowledged and asked, may deign to do so.

But if we were considering an earthly king, wouldn't we think this king lacking in compassion if he could help in cases of legitimate need, but did not? Would we not consider the king too much of an egotist if the condition of acting was the subject's worship? We might think such a condition would surely invite cajolery and flattery into the court in the hopes of gaining such a king's favor. Surely, if the king's concern was the governance of the realm toward peace and prosperity for all subjects, and if this peace and prosperity were within the power of the king, then the king would naturally see to this peace and prosperity. The king would not have to be asked.

I have developed each of these models in the extreme. I suspect that no Christian would use any of them so crassly as I have presented them. Yet I also suspect that given the supposition that an omniscient, omnipotent God really has no need of our prayers, one or more of these caricatures of prayer really does creep into our attitudes toward prayer and toward God. Insofar as they do, they jar our sensitivity of the greatness and graciousness of God and hinder our praying.

But we should turn once again to the image of God as king. By pushing the model a bit further, it may take us beyond its limitations and point to a way of imaging God that is more consistent with a God of presence. Suppose that the required peace and prosperity of the realm could only be gained in and through the subject's recognition of the king's rule. Perhaps an incognito governance simply would not work, and so the king makes petitioning the condition of action, despite the dangers of flattering sycophants this condition invites. In this case, the petition is itself a means to the end of the just kingdom. But the model, when pushed this far, begins to go beyond the notion of a self-sufficient God who acts unilaterally; it pushes toward a model of shared power within a context that is contingent upon mutual responsiveness. At this point, the image of a king may no longer be the best, in which case prayer as petitions to a king also fails as a model.

Suppose it is valid to say that recognition of God can enhance our ability to live lives of peace, justice, and beauty. Suppose that prayer, regardless of our images and our theologies, constitutes this recognition, and that the recognition is not necessarily limited to our intellects, but goes to the depths of ourselves. Suppose that prayer is our openness to the God who pervades the universe and therefore ourselves, and that prayer is also this God's openness to us. In such a case, prayer is not only for our sakes, but also for God's sake. This would make prayer essential to God as well as to ourselves. What if prayer increases the effectiveness of God's work with the world? God's invitation to us to pray—indeed, God's gracious command to pray—suggests the possibility that our prayers make a difference to God, and therefore might possibly make a difference to what God can do in the world.

This brings us to the basic supposition of a relational theology of prayer: *God works with the world as it is in*

order to bring it to where it can be. Prayer changes the way
the world is, and therefore changes what the world can be.
Prayer opens the world to its own transformation. To
develop this thesis, imagine that God is not totally
independent from the world—and indeed, from the image
of God brooding over the waters in Genesis, to God's
wooing of a people in the lore of Jewish history, to the
incredible nature imagery of the Psalms and wisdom
literature, to the intimate images of relationship between
God and the Jews in prophetic literature, to the story of
God's incarnational activity in the Gospels, to the images
of God's Spirit brooding over and through the church in
the epistles, to the culminating image of God's renewal of
all creation in Revelation, does not the Scripture itself contradict the notion of a God totally independent of the
world? Our texts portray a God deeply involved with the
world and its events, with God wooing the world to deeper
modes of community and caring, wooing us toward deeper
relation with one another and with God's own self. So
imagine, as the Scriptures suggest, that God is not independent of the world, but interdependent with the world.
Imagine that the God of the universe, like flowing water,
is in intimate relation with all elements throughout the
universe, and therefore with all our earth as well. Imagine
that God, in creative relation to the earth, woos the earth
so that it becomes a world, and woos the world in the
hope that it might yet become a peaceful and just reflection
of the divine image.

What would it mean for our understanding of
omnipotence if in fact God is interdependent with the
world? Omnipotence means, literally, *all power.* But given
the reality of the world with its many forms of existence,
omnipotence may be a self-contradictory term, even when
applied to God. To exist at all is to have some mode of
power, for existence is a power for being. There is energy

in every event of existing. Even the most minute form of existence pulsates with its being, radiating an energy that affects others. Existence is power by very definition. If, then, God creates a world, then that world has the power of its own existence. To be sure, its power may be dependent upon the initially creative power of God, but its power is nonetheless truly its own. It is itself, and it has power. But if many things exist, and each thing that exists has power simply through its existence, it is by definition impossible for any reality—even God—to have all the power there is. An omnipotent reality would have to be the *only* reality.

Think of power in relation to experience. True, we often feel a bit powerless, but is it not so that our powerlessness is a contrast to a deeper reality, which is our power of being? Each one of us feels the effects of others; others feel our own effects, for good or for ill. That each one of us exerts a mode of power is a given. If, then, the world sheerly through its existence has its own form of power, then we must contextualize the power of God. God's power is simply not all the power there is, not even if creation's power has its origins in divine power. In bringing a world into being, God has chosen to share power. This means that the power we experience is not illusory; it is our reality. God has power, but so does the world, and the world's power is as real as God's.

We can take this a step further by arguing that power is freedom. We exist, and our existence is power. Our power is certainly not absolute—it is relative, contextualized by the power of others, human and nonhuman, and by the circumstances of our social location, our histories. Sometimes our own power is overwhelmed by events beyond our control, whether within our own bodies as we experience our mortality, or by others, or by the environment. But even within the limitations and relativity of our power, we exercise our own power of existence with a relative degree of freedom. Our freedom is twofold. At the simplest level, freedom is the power to make choices. At a deeper level, freedom is the power to develop according to our own particular and unique giftedness. This latter form of freedom is deeply entwined with the freedom of choice, for through our daily choices we cumulatively form and bring our character to expression. So our power of being is exercised fundamentally through our freedom. Freedom and power are corollaries of one another.

God is also free, and insofar as God is Spirit, God's freedom is far deeper than our own, since God would not be constrained by physical conditions. But consider: God's freedom and God's power are not exercised in some totally isolated domain—and in fact only in such an imaginary domain could God's freedom and power be absolute. But the God we know in Jesus Christ is a God who is for us, with us, creating us and calling us. God woos us to become a people acting with God the Creator toward the well-being of the world.

But if we have a situation where God's power and freedom interact with our power and freedom, then we have a situation where God's power and freedom are limited by our own. Perhaps such a situation is the consequence of a divine choice made before the foundations of the world; perhaps it is simply the incredible dynamics of the way things have always been. Perhaps God has never been without some world, some universe—who can know? But the situation we experience today, for whatever cause, is one where God's freedom and power appear to be relational, existing in and through the fluid boundaries created through the freedom and power of the world.

To argue that God's power is so much greater than the world's that the world's power comes to nothing is to miss the point. There is an analogy between the way our own power is limited by the powers of others, and the way God's power is limited by the world. For example, we have much more power than that possessed by a delicate rose. We can use our greater power to nurture the flower—but we cannot bloom for it, it must bloom for itself; only the rose has that power. We can use our power simply to enjoy the flower, in which case our power and the rose's complement each other. Or we could destroy the flower—but such a use of power diminishes the power in the world, since it loses the power of the rose to bloom, and sacrifices our own power to nurture and to enjoy. So what is the value of our greater power? It gives possibilities for nurturance, enjoyment, and destruction. But it does not give us the power to be the rose.

Would it not be somewhat similar with God's power over us? Differences would remain, even as they do between us and the rose. Both we and the rose share physical existence, and perhaps—who knows?—we also share spiritual existence, but we do not seem to share conscious existence. This limits the kinds of relationship roses and people can have with each other. It also limits the kind of power we can exercise with each other. We imagine that between God and ourselves there is a sharing of conscious and spiritual existence, but not physical existence. This places limitations on our relationship and upon our respective powers. The greater power of God does not cancel the power of a living creature, even though God's power is greater than our own. The difference only contributes to the kind of relationship that our intermingled powers together can create.

Often we Christians have thought that the best relationship to God would be abrogation of our own power by pretending that we do not have it, or by treating it as something shameful, as if the very Godness of God depended upon no one other than God having any power that counted. But what would be so godly about that? Why is power such a determiner of godness? And if God indeed has totalitarian power, then the witness of history shouts out a story of divine abuse of power. If God has enough power to stop the horror of the many genocidal holocausts the world has devised, but does not do so, how is this godly? Perhaps our own obsession with power has led us to think it the best of divine compliments to attribute total power to God, but perhaps we are wrong.

In our great reluctance to give up the notion of total divine power we have said that God voluntarily chooses to limit God's power so that God can honor our own freedom. But even this is problematic. Is the freedom of the ethnic cleansers of greater value than the lives of those they murder? Even in human courts of justice we choose to limit the freedom of the criminal in order to protect the greater society! Why does God not do as much? I know of a young child who, in running across the street, was hit and killed by a drunk driver. Did God really prefer to stand by and watch, rather than interfere with the freedom of the drunkard? Could God not have overridden that drunk's freedom just long enough to keep him sober that night, or at least at home? What price freedom, if indeed God chooses to protect it at all costs! If God is omnipotent, independent of the world, capable of changing anything in the world at will, then God could have intervened not only in that child's death, but in every case of senseless slaughter. The untimely deaths happened, unhindered by the God who could have prevented them, but chose not to do so. Is our notion of the dependence of godness on total power, or omnipotence, worth such a price? Perhaps it is we, rather than God, who deem such power so important. What if it's the case that the world truly has power, and that this power can as easily be used against God as in conformity with God? Supposing not even God could deflect the slaughterers of this world? Are our choices then between a tyrant God and a wimp?

I suggest that the middle way is the relational God encountered in biblical texts, and that prayer in a universe with a relational God who shares power and freedom with a people is quite different from prayer in a universe where God can at will override all persons and situations. It feels riskier to be in a world where our power and freedom are real—there is a wistful preference for a sense that God is waiting in the wings to whomp on all evil, just waiting for the right moment—a right moment somehow always a bit too late for the victims of this world. Perhaps it is a riskier world, after all. But paradoxically enough, it seems to me that there is more hope in a riskier world than in that other.

So imagine with me the dynamics of relationship between God and the world. Think of it as a dance, whereby in every moment of existence God touches the world with guidance toward its communal good in that time and place, and that just as the world receives energy from God it also returns its own energy to God. God gives to the world and receives from the world; the world receives from God and gives to God, ever in interdependent exchange. Imagine this dance to be initiated by the everlasting God acting out of divine freedom, and therefore out of everlasting faithfulness—for if God is free, then God is free to act in consistency with God's own character. Thus every touch of God is a giftedness reflecting to some degree God's own character. But only to some degree. For if this dancing God truly relates to the manyness of the world, then God relates to the particularities of the world. God relates not to some ideal world, but to the reality of this world.

If such is the case, then God's touch to the world in every instant is contextualized not only by the divine character, but also by the conditions in the world that affect the way each element in the world can be. The world is always in the middle of its many stories, so that the reality of God's touch is in fact the conditioned nature of that touch. As the Quakers put it, God meets our condition. The drunk, for example, also receives the creative touch of God, and this touch reflects both the character of God *and* the reality of the alcoholic's life. Long ago this addict overrode God's call toward sobriety, and the overriding of the divine call becomes successively easier with the addiction. Faithfully God touches the addict in each moment, offering what good is possible—even though given the context the good may be barely recognizable as a good by an observer. The best, sometimes, is simply bad. But when one moves with that best, the next best may be a little better, and step by step, God offers modes of transformation. God's touch is conditioned by the world, and limited by the world, so that God must ever adapt divine possibilities to the reality of who we are becoming in the total movement of our lives.

God's touch is not only conditioned by who we are becoming, but also by our surroundings. Indeed, if God acted toward us in a totally noncontextualized manner, how could God's touch guide us given the fact that we, at least, are immersed in our contexts? If I am in a war-torn place, beleaguered by bombs and guns and hunger and cold, and if God touches me with possibilities that have nothing to do with the concreteness of my situation, how is God at all salvific for me? But in a relational, interdependent world, God not only gives to me and receives from me, but also gives and receives directly from every element in my environment. God *knows* my situation, better than I know it myself. And knowing my situation—my agony, my pain, my fear—God touches me where I am, offering me what forms of transformation are possible even in my dire circumstances. It may not look like much to me in terms of what I wish God could give me—but because God's touch meets my condition, it offers me hope.

How does God's touch come to me? In a relational, interdependent universe, God's touch is a directive energy flowing into me at the basic level of my existence, far deeper than my sensory perception, or my central nervous system, or my consciousness. God's energy meets and mingles with the energy of all other relations from my environment and my own embodiedness, so that I necessarily receive God's energy as a mediated touch, received through the material energy of all my being. The peculiarity that I call "I" responds with whatever degree of freedom I may have in each moment—and freedom is a variable, not a constant—to choose my own becoming. In such a relational world, one is in interdependent relation to God whether or not one is conscious of it—and in fact, in such a world the very constancy of God's presence and the subliminal nature of that presence suggest that we are so habituated to God's presence that we do not notice it. God is an ever-faithful presence, ever touching us toward our good.

But if this is an interdependent world, then just as surely as we receive from God, God receives from us. Who we are, in every newly becoming moment, is received by God, known by God, felt by God. If we receive from the energy of God, howsoever contextualized to our situation that touch may be, then it is so that God also receives from us. To exist is to exert some influence, so that who we are has an effect upon how others are. We are each a source of power, of energy, affecting others—and not only other persons, but as we know too well today, also our environment. All of existence is an interrelational, interdependent dance of mutual effect, action and reaction, making a difference. The energy that is each of us affects other persons and the environment to degrees that in an earlier age we would have thought improbable. Today, in an age of relativity physics, we learn that every pulse of energy actually has effects throughout the universe. Is it so improbable, then, to suppose that God is affected by us, too? How could the God of the relational universe be the only reality untouched by our energy, impervious to who we are? If God is affected by us, then prayer takes on the awesome character of being one way that we can shape the energy God receives from us.

Imagine, then, that God experiences our own energy in every moment of our completion. God—the God of the universe—is touched by who we are. My mother, who was not given to pious thoughts, once spoke in exasperation to me about her neighbor Louise. Louise was a fervent fundamentalist who prayed about everything, including her daily menu. Foolishness! said my mother. Why would the God of the universe care about what she has for lunch? Her image of God, of course, was something like that King of the Universe, with many important things to do, most delegated to underlings. Far down on the scale of universal concerns was tiny little Louise, preparing her shopping list. But the image of God I am proposing is of a God pervasively present, like water, to every nook and cranny of the universe, continuously wooing the universe toward continuous transformation toward its greater good. A King of the Universe could not possibly care about Louise's little world—but a God of the Universe could. And does. I am proposing an image of a God who interacts with the universe not partially, but *totally*. Such a God creatively gives to and receives from all forms of existence. Only a God could do that. A king, of course, never could.

So then: God gives to the world and receives from the world; the world receives from God and gives to God. God gives creative and suggestive energy to the world, and the world gives the results of what it has done with this energy back to God. Prayer in such a world is an openness to God's own creative energy, and to the good that God intends for us. It is also an offering back to God, giving God the gift of ourselves.

If the God to whom we pray is a relational God, pervasively present in the universe, what is this praying that opens us to God and gives us to God? What is this praying that changes the way the world is, and therefore changes what God can do with the world? We have already established that God works with the world in the context of the world's own power, its own freedom. God's creative power works with the world's creative power—and sometimes against the world's resistant power. For the world can resist God. It cannot eliminate God, and it cannot change God's self-chosen character; it cannot defeat the divine faithfulness, and it cannot rid itself of the divine presence. But the world can distort the guidance of God; it can refuse the possibilities given for its transformation. It can reject God moment by moment. Alternatively, the world can open itself to God, becoming a co-laborer with God, exercising its influence in conjunction with God's greater aim toward deeper modes of human communities of caring. The world can respond to God in love, and know its own love to be a uniquely creative reflection of God's deeply wooing love. And whether we respond to God in rejection or in love, God inexorably experiences our response—God inexorably experiences us.

We are told in our tradition that God bids us to pray, invites us to pray, inspires us to pray. If it is truly an interdependent world, existing in interdependence not only within itself but also with the ever-creating God, then God's call to us to pray is neither whimsical nor irrelevant to God's work with the world. It is not a manner of receiving compliments, nor is it a reminder service informing God of what needs to be done in the world. Rather, prayer is

God's invitation to us to be willing partners in the great dance of bringing a world into being that reflects something of God's character.

Our images of God can help or hinder our praying, but the God who is more than any image can adequately portray continues to inspire us to pray, hearing us more deeply than our faltering words, and using our prayers in ways that go far beyond what we can ever know this side of eternity. I've proposed images of water, of touch, and of dance to suggest to us the relational reality of the God to whom we pray. But finally, while images help us and we do indeed pray with some image of God in mind, it is not to the image that we pray. Nor is it an image that receives our prayers. It is God's own self.

CHAPTER THREE

Conditions of Prayer

In the previous chapter I suggested that God works with the world as it is to bring it toward what it can be. Prayer changes the way the world is, and therefore changes what the world can be. Prayer makes a difference to what God can do in and with the world. This follows from a relational understanding of God, and the dynamic implications for prayer given the interdependence between God and the world. In this chapter I will discuss the core elements of our communion with God in prayer. These conditions of prayer include the dynamics of prayer, release of prayer, honesty in prayer, and the language of prayer.

If God exists relationally, in interdependence with the world, then the conditions for communion with God always exist. Since God is the omnipresent one, these conditions exist for all beings. The effects of God's presence include guidance toward what each reality might become within its particular context. Divine guidance is limited by our condition—our histories, our prejudices, our attitudes, our openness, our closedness: our selves. We take this guidance into ourselves, and dispose of it as we choose. The guidance is not emblazoned with notification that it is God who so guides us—to the contrary, it is more like an impulse toward a best responsiveness to whatever our situation might be. The impulse is deeper than our immediate consciousness, so that we do not necessarily notice either it or its giver. But we experience its effects.

There is a return movement, too, making this a dance of the divine presence. We receive from God, whether consciously or not, and we give to God, whether consciously or not. God touches us: but to touch is to be touched, so that God is also touched by us. Oh, we need not know it! But in this giving and receiving world, God not only gives to us, but receives from us, and we not only receive from God, we give to God. And what do we give, but ourselves? For who we are and how we are is received by God in every moment. If God guides us by giving us possibilities for our existence, we give God back the actualization of those possibilities—or at least, the actualization of how we ourselves have transformed a possibility into the continuous becoming of ourselves. Sometimes what we have done with God's possibility is so changed as to be totally unlike that initially God-given impulse. But whatever we have done with it, we return it to God. As God experiences us, God fashions for us yet another possibility that we once again may transform to whatever degree, once again giving the results back to God. And this happens again, and again, and again. The dance is repeated with every element of existence. One could call it the creativity of God, or the omnipresence of God, or the persuasive power of God. But whatever we may say of it, it is the great communion with God, and the basis for prayer.

We could put it in more theological language, and say that the initial impulse that we receive from God is "prevenient grace," the power of God that always goes before us, like a light in the darkness. And we could say that our internalization of this impulse is our acceptance of the graciousness of God that leads to our conversion, or our growth in goodness, or our sanctification. And we might note that God's reception of us is a continuous judgment, transformation and salvation that affects the shape of God's continuous graciousness toward us. But whether we use traditional theological language or relational language, we establish the framework of prayer.

This framework for a relationship with God exists for all, but at unconscious levels. Prayer is the act of bringing our moment-by-moment connectedness to God into our consciousness. Through prayer we actually address God as if our doing so made some difference to God, which of course it does. Because the impulses God gives us are conditioned by where and when and who and how we are, these impulses are affected when we become one who prays. Prayer opens us to God's presence and/or guidance, and thus shifts our ability to receive whatever guidance is appropriate for ourselves and the communities of which we are a part.

Prayer also opens us to the possibility of change, with the direction of that change oriented by God's wisdom relative to us. Truly, only a God could be this for every element in the universe—and the growth of our knowledge of the complexity of the universe forces us also to acknowledge the enormous complexity of God. Only a God could be so intentionally present to all things at all times.

How can we be sure that in our act of praying we are releasing our prayers to this God of the universe? Prayer is to God. In this day of reductionism there is sometimes a tendency to think of prayer as a psychological sorting of things over in our minds. Some think of prayer as little more than a meditation that quiets us down, something like a good nap, in the midst of our busyness. Too easily we think of prayer as really talking to ourselves, just thinking things over. But prayer is not to ourselves, it is to God, and we must take that seriously.

Certain things follow from the fact that prayer is directed to God. It means that we do not own our prayers. We have given them to God. Sometimes our temptation is to hang onto prayer, clutching our prayers as if they were still ours. But in this relational world, it is God who prompts our praying in the first place, in which case the very fact that we can pray is already a gift from God. The actual praying is in return our gift back to God. Thus it is important to release our prayers into the divine keeping.

I experienced an image of this release during my participation in a baptismal service and celebration for a friend's child in Germany. Baptisms in Germany, it appears, are splendid occasions, lasting all day. Following the service, the dinner, and the festivities, the guests were invited to write wishes for the infant, and to place these wishes inside balloons that were then filled with helium (unfortunately, we did not yet know the negative environmental impact of such balloons). With balloons in hand, we all went outside the church, and at the signal we released our balloons, watching them rise first collectively, and then separately, till they looked like so many bits of colored confetti in the sky. Who knows where they went, or if anyone found those wishes, released so into the world! Prayer is not a balloon, and the God to whom we pray is not "up there," but the process of releasing our prayers is not unlike that process of releasing those balloons. Since our prayers are given to God, we must let go of them, trusting God to do with those prayers what God can and will. God prompts our praying, receives our praying, and works with our praying. To take seriously the fact that it is God to whom we pray, and not ourselves, calls for us to pray and release. We trust that God prompts the prayer for purposes that are deeper than we can know. Thus we release each prayer to the God who receives it.

Releasing prayer to God does not mean we cannot continue to pray for a person or situation deep within our concerns—quite to the contrary. Sometimes we are so troubled that we cannot cease from praying again and again, for we have no rest apart from prayer. To release prayer does not mean that one is not allowed to pray more than once on a topic. But there is a difference between hoarded prayer and released prayer. Hoarded prayer insists upon its program, and is not willing for God to do other with the prayer than that which is dictated in the prayer. This is truly prayer, but it is not freeing prayer. Released prayer is more like a breathing, it takes the same depth of one's heart's concern to God, offering it and releasing it, offering it and releasing it. To release prayer is to count on the fact that it is God who receives and deals with this prayer, not oneself.

To release our prayers is to recognize that we do not control what God does with our prayers. In a sense, it is none of our business. Our business is to pray and to be sensitive to any way God might use us in response to our prayers. But even then, we cannot assume that any perceived answer is the sum total of what God does with our prayers—they are, after all, given to God, even though our common use of language refers to "our" prayers. And if we have no control over what God is going to do with our prayers, then we don't have enough information to know whether God has said "yes" or "no" to our prayers. Prayer is not like a true/false quiz, restricting God to yes or no. God uses our prayers in light of a context only partially known to us, but fully known to God. God matches the resources of the divine nature to the capacities of the world for its own transformation. Sometimes we do indeed see what seems to us to be the fruit of our praying—but we do not know what other prayers were woven along with ours into God's doing, nor dare we assume that what we see is all of what God is doing with the prayers we have offered. It is God to whom we pray, and only God knows the full effectiveness of what those prayers make possible. Thus we release our prayers to God.

Releasing prayer also involves the recognition that we do not fully know the condition about which we pray. Often we bring to God a very specific prescription, or a most explicit request. When one we love is ill, we pray quite specifically for healing. But we never know the fullness of that person or that situation—and for all our specificity, we never dare assume that our specificity exhausts the possibilities for good that in fact may be the case. Thus we pray within the tension that although we name the concern, we know it to be but partially known by us. Indeed, the function of praying after the manner of Jesus in Luke 22 with "not my will, but thine be done" is that our limited perspective hides the full nature of every situation from us. And so we bring our concerns to God in prayer, releasing them to the fuller concerns of God. Prayers, even when specific, are offered with an openness toward well-being for the ones for whom we pray, and then the prayers are released.

Releasing prayer to God constitutes the freedom of prayer. It is the giving over of concern that paradoxically makes the concern bearable. Releasing prayer means that resources more than my own are involved, and a carer greater than myself cares more. This awareness can remove the constraining power of those burdening things that we bring to God in prayer. In releasing the prayer, we to some extent release the burden as well, and consequently live in the freedom that is one of God's gifts in prayer.

Often we take prayer for granted, and perhaps that is well and good—it is the "least common denominator," that one activity that democratizes the church. Prayer knows no hierarchy—lay and clergy, young and old, high intelligence or low, healthy or ill—*all* have access to God in prayer. And perhaps because all can pray, we who somewhat prefer our hierarchical way of doing things rather downgrade prayer to a perfunctory sort of thing. Humans, it seems, are afflicted with a tendency to value those things most highly that only a few can do—but all can pray. Prayer, then, is extraordinarily ordinary. And this can blind us to the awesome reality that in prayer, we are dealing with God. Prayer is to God.

Because prayer is to God, honesty is an essential element of prayer. Quite simply, if God knows me better than I know myself, what point is there in pretending I am other than I am before God? Prayer is not the place for pretended piety; prayer is the place for getting down to brass tacks. Emotions that one might hesitate to express in converse with others are appropriately expressed in prayer. To be human is to experience the full range of emotions, whether anger, outrage, despair, depression, grief, impatience, pain, cynicism, jadedness, hopelessness, unbelief. And being human, we experience each of these emotions to some degree at some point in our lives, as well as those happier emotions we may feel freer to name as our own.

Have you never been very angry with God? There are times when our sense of justice is outraged, or when someone we love is in horrible pain, and we cry out to God for relief. But the injustice or the pain continues, even as we pray for redress. We pray, and release the praying, and continue to experience the assault on our spirits by the situation of great grief. Has your soul never, like mine, screamed its rage at God for seemingly doing nothing? Sometimes I have an image of beating my fists against the chest of God, sobbing like a comfortless child. We cry out for a well-being whose fullness seems ever more illusory, and feel anger toward the God who does not give it. Ancient images of God as the one who can do all things, interfering in any circumstance, crowd out images of a God who works with the world as it is, and in the clash of images I cry against the withholding God, sharing my pain with the God who is present. It is all right to share rage with the God who understands it, receives it, and returns instead that other image: Underneath are the everlasting arms.

So we are called to honesty in prayer, regardless of the state of our emotional well-being. God receives us as we are, and how we are is no surprise to God. God, being continuously present to us, has no doubt noticed how we are before we take notice of it ourselves. Thus we might as well acknowledge our true state when we pray. We pray to God from where we are, not from where we consider we should be. And God, who knows us where we are, can lead us to where we can be.

This leads to the final general condition of prayer, which is the matter of language. What words do we use; what words are adequate for addressing the God of the universe? I am speaking now specifically about personal and informal prayers, not yet the liturgical prayers of the church. Since it is God to whom we pray, I suspect that all language and no language is appropriate. Does God have a language? We are imbued with the image that God has a word—but this word is a person, not a paragraph. What is God's native tongue?

Wilshire United Methodist Church in Los Angeles is an inner-city church where four major languages are spoken by the congregation: Korean, Spanish, Tongan, and English. The church has five pastors, who are respectively Tongan,

Hispanic, Korean, African-American, and Euro-American. There are many worship services, with some being oriented primarily to the customs of one ethnicity, and others being joint. When I attended one of the latter, I noted that the bulletin was printed with all four languages set up in parallel columns. The pastor preached in a combination of Japanese and English; summaries of his sermon were printed in the bulletin in the other languages. The custom, I was told, was that whichever pastor preached did so in his or her own tongue, with printed translations provided. At the conclusion of the service, the joint choir—with more than 50 percent Korean members—sang Handel's "Hallelujah Chorus"—in Spanish. The power of this service was, among other things, the relativization of language. Which is God's native tongue? Each of them, of course—and none of them.

I suspect that God hears us from a place deeper than language. Perhaps every language is translated back into God's language of the Spirit. Have you sometimes had the experience of meeting someone, and feeling as if you already knew the person, even though you've not yet said anything particularly meaningful to her? Have you not felt some flow of spirit between you and a stranger, as if you knew each other before you met? Perhaps whatever "language" it is that communicates in that meeting is more akin to the language God hears in our prayers than our vocabulary and our grammar.

The point of this is that one does not have to learn a "language of prayer" for nonliturgical prayer. All language is appropriate, because God translates all our language into that of the Spirit. Are we not told something similar to this in the eighth chapter of Romans? Because of this deeper-than-language communication, the clumsiest of prayers in our native speech, translated by God, may be offerings of sheer beauty in the poetry of the Spirit. Alternatively, it is possible that the most elegant of prayers might be but shabby things in that divine translation. We ourselves are not fit to judge—but God is. God receives us from levels deeper than our words, beyond the mere hearing of speech. And so all communication—oral or signed, refined or clumsy, unschooled or schooled, is God's language; none need fear that he or she cannot rightly pray. Our spirits meet God's Spirit in prayer, with a communication much deeper than words.

There is that other language of Christian prayer, the liturgy of the church. Developed over long centuries, this language expresses the corporate spirituality of a people, and gives speech to those who otherwise struggle to find words. Such prayers have the great benefit of bringing to expression the communal context of all our prayers—for whether we pray personally or in a congregation, we pray in and through the community of which we are a part. The community has formed us, shaping our spirituality to its own contours. Thus even when we pray individually, our praying reflects a traditional way of addressing God. We are communal in our individuality. To pray in the language of the community brings this aspect of ourselves into expression before God.

To pray in the explicit language of the community also provides a deep channel for those emotions that so easily overflow our shallow banks. The Psalms in particular speak the full gamut of our feelings, and give us a voice for that which otherwise defies expression. And when we speak in a language first developed by others, it is as if their own saying and our saying merge; we become one with them, and they with us, and together we find the power of speech. Further, a great multitude of persons have prayed these same prayers before us. As we pray them too, we become more deeply united with all these others who are our brothers and sisters in the Spirit. Together, we voice these feelings to God. Together we can say what feels too strong to say as an individual alone. And the channel for these feelings has been deepened with every saying, down all the long years.

There is an additional sweetness when we pray the Jewish Psalms. When we Christians pray the Psalms, we pray from the formative spirituality of another people who wrote those Psalms so many generations ago. As we join them in this praying, they become a part of our own reality. In writing down their prayers to God, the Jews gave themselves not only to God, but also to all those who would follow them by lifting again the prayers they first voiced and sang. They gifted a people beyond themselves and even beyond their own tradition with some of their own spirit. And if God is omnipresent, breathing life into all peoples, generating many communal stories, then God, however personal God may seem, is never private to oneself or one's own community. Praying the Psalms gently speaks to us of wider communities than our own Christian community, of other peoples who belong to God, of other languages breathed in the presence of God's own Spirit. The Psalms, even while speaking of and through and in our most personal of feelings, lift us to that wider community of God, joining us to it even as we are deeply ourselves.

This language of communal prayer, be it the Psalms or the liturgies of prayer books or worship services, interweaves with the more informal language uttered in our personal communion with God. Each form of language has its place—but all forms of language fall silent—or come to their fullest expression—as God's own receiving makes them God's own.

CHAPTER FOUR

Intercessory Prayer

What happens in our prayers for others? Sometimes the theologian in all of us is not content simply with statements and practice; we have the notion that we must know "how it works." I often remember with amusement the climactic scene from *The Wizard of Oz*: The wizard, Dorothy, and Toto are in the basket of the balloon, ready to leave for Kansas, when Toto leaps out, and Dorothy after him. At that moment the balloon begins to rise. "Come back, come back," calls Dorothy, to which the wizard replies, "I can't! I don't know how it works!" A sense of "how it works" will enhance our use of the rather astounding privilege of prayer.

I have suggested that God has an effect upon how and what this universe is and is becoming, and that this universe has a return effect upon God. In this dance of relation, imagine what prayer might be like from God's perspective. Do not shrink from such an imagining, for all theology spins from the power we have to think beyond ourselves. The God who is more than all our theologies can handle our imaginings, and perhaps strengthens us through them. So, then, imagine this dance between God and the universe as it might be from God's perspective.

First, look more closely into how relationships affect us, as human beings. We are continuously affected by that which is more than ourselves, whether personal, societal, or environmental. Whom we know, and how intimately we know them, affects who we are. We are not totally determined by these relationships, for we have the ability to respond to each out of some degree of freedom. Over time our character develops out of the interplay between those things that influence us and our freely chosen responses. And just as we have been affected by those to whom we relate, even so they are affected by our response to them. Relationships create an ongoing dance of influence, response, and influence once again, and in the process, we develop and express our own characters.

Imagine that it is somewhat like this for God. God, too, has a freely chosen character from everlasting to everlasting. But God's character, like ours, is expressed in responsiveness to relationships throughout the universe—for there would be nothing to which God did not relate. God receives the influences given by each relationship, and responds to each. Imagine that God's own deepest character is freely manifested according to the various conditions of all sorts of people and things in all sorts of places. God "meets our condition," as the Quakers say, and this "meeting" is shaped by God in response to each aspect of creation God touches.

To imagine how God experiences intercessory prayer under these circumstances, consider that since God relates to each aspect of creation in all of creation's varied time frames, then no matter how remote two persons may be from each other, there is a sense in which they "meet" in God. The same God receives the influences of both of them, and responds to both of them, according to God's own character and to the particular circumstances of each. This would be true for strangers who think of God in entirely different ways; it would also be true for the dearest of friends. If God responsively feels every aspect of creation, wherever it may be, then all things and all persons eventually meet in God through God's feelings of them and for them.

In order to clarify the implications for intercessory prayer, let me describe for you one person's situation. I went to Korea, and there met a man in considerable need whose condition touched my heart. I know only a little of his full situation, but God knows it all. It appears to me that the man was treated unjustly, suffering grievously through his mistreatment. In every moment of this man's existence God feels his pain, along with the fullness of its causes, including whatever responsibility the man himself contributed to his condition. And God touches him with an impulse toward his own transformative good. That touch comes unfailingly, even in the midst of the man's struggle with the consequences of the injustice he received. God doesn't turn the injustice into pretense; God doesn't render it invisible; God doesn't suggest to the man that he simply override the injustice as if it didn't exist. Should God so act, then God would not be meeting this man's real condition. Instead, God weaves together all the circumstances of the man's world, blends them with what is yet possible from the depths of God's own character in relation to these circumstances, and offers the consequent possibility to the man as an impulse for his good. What

God gives him comes from the fullness of what the man is dealing with, how the man is dealing with it, and God's own faithful response.

What this means is that the man's good is limited by his circumstances. He is hedged in, as it were, by the reality of his harsh situation, and God must work with that situation as it is. Insofar as the man's associates view him with ill will, God must take that ill will into consideration—into the divine weaving—as God works toward that man's true good. Insofar as he has lost his job and struggles to buy daily bread for himself and his family, this, too, is part of the material with which God must work. Given the fullness of these circumstances, there is only so much good that can be offered, for the situation is bad. What God can do for him—for us—is reality based, not magically based. The transforming good that God can offer the man must meet the harshness of his conditions, even though tempered as much as possible by the divine character.

I am in America—separated by time, geography, and culture from this Korean. But in God we meet. When I pray for his well-being, I make myself relevant to his condition. It means that as God weaves together the circumstances of that man in order to fashion his best possibility for the next moment of his becoming, my praying offers new stuff for the weaving. The ill will of others is countered to some extent by the goodwill of those who pray for him. And this goodwill becomes part of his relevant world. Since God works with the world as it is in order to bring it to what it can be, intercessory praying changes what that world is relative to that one for whom we pray, and that change is for the good. It therefore adds to what God can then offer that one, releasing more of the divine resources toward the good that God can then use.

When I pray for this man's well-being, even though I am greatly separated from him in time and place, even though he is an acquaintance newly met rather than a long-time friend or family member, my praying for him joins me with him in God. This relational theology indicates that we become one with those for whom we pray within God's own being, for we meet in God. It is God who feels this man's condition; it is God who feels my own condition in my praying for him; it is God who weaves me into this man's welfare. It matters not that I have no experiential consciousness of this—nor should I, for it is within God's own self that this weaving happens. God feels the world as it is, unifying that world within God's own nature in order to offer good to the world individually in all its aspects. How the world is unified within God depends upon God's own feelings of each part of the world's relevance to all other parts, and upon God's gracious ability to combine the world toward its good in and through God's own nature. Praying for another's well-being allows God to weave us into that other's well-being. In this manner we become part of those for whom we pray, and they become part of us.

All things relate to all other things. In this interdependent world, everything that exists experiences to some degree the effects of everything else. We are so constituted that very, very little of all this relationality makes it to our conscious awareness. But we are connected, nonetheless; it is sure. Praying lifts these loose connections to our conscious awareness in the context of God's presence. We begin to feel an echo of that divine meeting and weaving, no matter how distant the one for whom we pray. Through prayer, we can begin to experience the relationships that are otherwise too subliminal for us to notice. Intercessory prayer is a place of meeting, within God and to a far less intense degree, within the world.

There is another implication of this meeting in God when our prayers involve us in supportive intercession for the work of others, whether near or far. As a Christian church we have a mission to be channels of God's love in this world, acting toward the alleviation of misery both by working to change structures that contribute to misery, and by administering the "cup of cold water" in Christ's name. We are to do these deeds not silently, but as those who speak of the love we have received from God through Christ: we share our stories, ourselves, in our doing. The Christian gospel calls us to proclamation in word and deed.

The tasks within our mission are enormous, as enormous as the problems of the world. Where there is greed, exploitation, hatred, injustice, pain, misery, or hardship of any kind in this earth there is a call to Christian witness. And Christian witness is a "deeded" word, and a "worded" deed; proclamation is word and deed. Clearly there is more to do than can be done by any one person. But as Christians we are called to enter into God's caring for the world. How can we do this, save through prayer?

While we prayerfully do the small task given to each of us, we can also enter into prayer for the mission of the church as a whole, and of its many members who, like us, are called to their own part of its mission. Instead of being limited to tasks that are in the range of our capabilities, prayer enables us to participate in the tasks of others, tasks which our own talents could never equip us to do. Then again, of course, there is no one who can do our own task in the same way that we can do it. Others, praying for us, participate in our work. Prayer then becomes the weaving together of all the various works involved in the mission of the church, making them one and us one, even in such great diversity. Prayer is the weaving of things, making us participants in one another's work, strengtheners to each other in our work, through the grace and power of God.

Were the God-world relation one where there were absolutely no limitations on God, then the universe would be a place where intercessory prayer would be absolutely unnecessary. But in a God-world relation of interdependence, where the world's power must be taken into account, where God's power is exercised in the form of possibilities that the world has the power to reject, then intercessory prayer is of utmost importance. It's not just that *we* need to pray—it's that God needs us to do the praying. Our prayers actually make a difference to what God can do.

God works with the world as it is. Quite simply, prayer changes the "isness" of the world. A world where there is this specific praying going on is not the same as a world where this praying is not going on. And the God who is always working with the world takes every opportunity within the world to influence it for its own good. For this reason, I am convinced that it is God's own self who prompts us to pray, and that when God needs resources for any particular situation, God will give an impulse toward prayer to those open to such an impulse so that their praying may make a difference to what God can give in yet another place.

God's touch upon our lives often takes the form of a call to us to pray so that we ourselves become a new opening for God's power in the world. Consider the horrible human penchant to slaughter those whom we do not perceive to be of our own kind. We assume that God does not will the slaughter of people, and that since God receives from every element of the world, God, as well as the slaughtered, experiences the pain of the hatred and its killing power. What can God do against human intransigence? We have long since learned that God is not a Thor, hurling thunderbolts in indignant retaliation. God works against the world's resistance. But when we pray for the well-being of those involved in dreadful bloodshed, even when we do not personally know these peoples, do we not give the God who works contextually more to work with? By our active caring, exercised through our prayers, have we not to some degree changed the context? Though we are at a distance, though we are relatively insignificant in the politics and hatreds of amassed power, though we have no control over foreign powers, yet we are not helpless. For God wills well-being and is a present force toward what forms of well-being are possible in any situation, even in the horror of military madness. When we pray we open ourselves to God's will toward well-being. The direct resistance toward well-being that God deals with in any strife is countered by our own openness toward that specific well-being. In a relational world, our caring directed toward others turns us into part of the context within which God works toward the other's good. Even though we are at a distance, our prayers change what is possible. For God is never at a distance.

A relational God, then, depends upon our prayers. But in a world of interdependence, we must recognize that God may use us in answer to our prayers. When we offer ourselves to God though prayers of intercession, whether for strangers we have never met in a distant country, for acquaintances, or for those we know more intimately, we do so realizing that God works through the world for the world. Through prayer, we open ourselves to conformity with God's great will. And if God touches us at every moment of our lives with directive energy, and if our will joins God's will in a care toward a particular personal or social situation for well-being, then there is no guarantee that God will not use us to bring about some aspect of that well-being. We risk being used by God as answers to our own prayers.

I experienced something of this some years ago when the movement against apartheid in South Africa was gaining momentum in America. I had prayed for justice and well-being in that country, of course, but never thought of any other mode of help. I had just moved to Washington, D.C., to become the dean at Wesley Theological Seminary, and I encountered an activist faculty. Scarcely a month had gone by since my arrival when the faculty voted to demonstrate at the South African embassy, even though this demonstration entailed civil disobedience. As the new dean, I felt bound to abide by the vote of the faculty, and to join the demonstration, but inwardly I was horrified. What? Get *arrested*? It filled me with terror, for it was the early days of these protests, and not yet apparent that those who demonstrated would not be sued, fined, and/or imprisoned. I moaned and groaned inwardly in my wimpish condition; I knew neither bravery nor courage as the appointed day came. Enhancing my shame at my cowardice was the knowledge that those for whom the demonstration was called faced not embarrassment, but torture and death. When they protested their deprivation of liberty and well-being, they received no courtesies. Compared to them, what did I or the faculty risk? For all this, I did not want to join the demonstration, and had it not been for the vote of the faculty, I would not have participated. I had no wish to defy the law.

But go I did, and to my horror it appeared that as dean, I was the leader. So I led the march, presented our petition at the embassy door, and stood with the others as we sang the songs of freedom. Because we ignored the warnings of the police to leave, we were eventually arrested, handcuffed, and driven to the police station to be fingerprinted, and eventually—to my enormous relief—released because the embassy chose not to sue. And so I returned to my home at the seminary, grateful at having "done my duty" unscathed, and at the same time muttering that it was all useless symbolism. After all, what difference did it make that I in America had done this foolish thing that not only paled in the face of what persons actually experienced in South Africa, but almost made a mockery of their great sacrifices?

Five months later the letter came. As dean, I was the one to receive it. Tears flowed down my cheeks as I read the letter from a pastor in South Africa, thanking us at Wesley Theological Seminary for what we had done. He had read of our protest, he said, and shared it with his congregation, and he could not say what courage it had given them to know that we, too, stood with them. It gave them a new boldness in their efforts, he said, as he thanked us in the name of God. And I wept.

The easiness of our prayers for these unknown people had become the hardness of action, even though that action was indeed a very tiny and insignificant part of the full drama of South Africa. But by the grace of God, it *did* become a part of it. Our actions were but a drop when an ocean was needed, but we were called to be that "drop." And we became part of a mighty ocean. These years later I see in wonder the ultimate fruit of all that has happened in that country of miracles. By the faithfulness of God, prayer has played a part in the empowerment of a people, the raising up of leaders, and some degree of resolution in the struggle toward a more just government.

Be careful for what you pray, for God may use you in addressing those things for which you pray, even though you are at a distance. Prayer creates a channel in the world through which God can unleash God's will toward well-being. Prayer puts you in the way of the channel, and you will become a part of God's rolling waters.

It is relatively easy to enter into intercessory prayer for causes or persons that engage our care, but we are bidden by the teachings of Jesus Christ to pray not only for our friends, but for our enemies. This would also be easy if in fact we were always open and loving to those whom we have reason to consider our enemies, but the reality is that we often return the feelings of enmity. In cases where the perceived enemy is a different country or ethnic group, then we easily demonize the enemy so as to more "righteously" destroy in a "just" war. In cases of personal injury, our natural attitude is to hope that the other will suffer even as he or she has made us suffer. In other cases the injury has been violation of an innocent one, such as in child abuse, and our feelings toward the one who has so violated the dear child are rage and indignation. We do not wish this person's well-being! When we are victims of crimes, we tend most often to will the ill-being of the violators.

But we are called to pray for our enemies. How shall we enter into this mode of intercessory prayer, and why? Isn't it enough that God will deal with them according to God's own wisdom? Why must we be involved at all? Our preference, in all charity, is to be far removed from that other, as if that other did not exist! We hardly notice or care that this is almost analogous to psychic murder.

There is a meeting in God that is heightened by earthly relevance, and whether we like it or not, the act of injury itself creates relevance. How we are makes a difference in how that other can be, and how the other is makes a difference in how we can be, for God works with the world as it is in order to lead it to where it can be. We are bidden to pray for the well-being of the offender and, in fact, the offender's well-being can increase the well-being of ourselves and those we love. Think of it! The injurer's well-being is also violated by the injury inflicted on others, for this is an impoverishment of his or her spiritual well-being. The injurer's well-being is transformation, and the transformation of the injurer bodes well for those who would yet be violated if there were no transformation. Ah, but we hate this one, and while we would begrudgingly admit transformation as well-being, we prefer they suffer as we have suffered first! How then do we obey the injunction to pray?

"Forgive us our trespasses, even as we forgive those who trespass against us." To forgive is to will the well-being of the other, and to live accordingly. We must pray for the other's well-being, even through gritted teeth, in the honesty of our souls. Sometimes the prayer is as crude as "Oh God, I wish they would rot in hell, but I pray for their well-being anyway, and ask you to forgive my own evil wishes even though I prefer to keep on wishing them; God help us both. Amen." There is seldom great release in such praying, since we are in the grip of hatred. But my experience is that responding to my wishes for vengeance with a prayer for the other's well-being actually begins to release me from my own participation in hatred and transform me. God universally desires well-being, and God desires my enemy's well-being. Should I not be in conformity with God's own great will toward well-being?

There is an odd sense wherein to continue in hatred is to perpetuate the crime, to continue to make it present in our emotional lives. Sometimes this is occasioned by the permanent effects of the initial crime—a murder removes the dear one forever from our family table, an infidelity ruins a marriage, a theft can result in financial ruin. The crime itself ensures that it will effectively deprive us of future good. But to continue in hatred is to block the transforming power of God that can lead us even through this tragic condition. To pray for the well-being of the violator gives God more to work with not only in dealing transformatively with the violator, but also in our own healing. We are called to pray for the well-being of those who despitefully use us, and in the process our own will can be transformed to become a reflection of God's will. The prayer that begins begrudgingly can slowly become a willing prayer, till at last we know the release of being one with God in praying for the other's well-being.

In such prayers—and indeed in all prayers—it is best not to dictate to God precisely what the form of well-being can be. We must release the prayers to God, and let God fill in the blanks, for only God knows the fullness of the circumstances. In releasing these prayers we nonetheless remain open to any impulse toward our own actions, for prayers are living things, affecting our attitudes and actions in the world. But on the whole it is safest to leave the prayer with God, releasing not only the prayer, but ourselves to a new future.

There are as many modes of intercessory prayer as there are modes of caring in the world. Often our prayers of intercession do not involve situations of dire need at all, but merely the ongoing condition of love. We pray for our family, our friends, our communities, lifting them before God in love, wanting for them all the rich goodness of life. We live in the paradox of praying for their good and only their good, even while we know that to be human is to hurt—it is not possible and perhaps not even desirable that we should go through life knowing no harm. So our prayer for their good is not necessarily for their protection from all harm; this would be humanly impossible. We pray for a good that includes their openness to the transforming love of God that brings them always into resurrection life, no matter what pains they may experience. We pray for the well-being of those we love.

In praying for their well-being, we are sometimes specific, but more often not. In faith, we do not know enough to be specific, for the fullness of another's circumstance, even those we most deeply love, is more than we are capable of knowing. But God knows. Remembering that all language in prayer is translated into God's own knowing, words become particularly insignificant, and so we pray instead through images. We "see" the face of the other, holding it in our heart with a yearning for that person's well-being, offering this fullness to God as prayer. We visualize the one for whom we pray in our minds or hearts or wherever such visualizing takes place, and open ourselves to God's will for that one's well-being.

Finally, it may not be our images alone any more than it is our words alone that constitute our prayers, but, rather, ourselves. The real prayer is the one who prays, the "prayer." In prayer we open ourselves to conformity with God's will toward well-being relative to a particular person, place, or time. God's will for that well-being is echoed or mirrored in our own will for that well-being, creating in the mirroring an image of God in us. Our whole being then becomes communion with God, so that we, the praying ones, become our prayers. In this communion, we offer ourselves for God's use in working the well-being we both ardently desire. And God will so use us, in ways not always given to our knowing.

CHAPTER FIVE

Prayers for Healing

Perhaps the intercessory prayers we offer more than any other—certainly in public settings—are prayers for those who are ill. What happens in this praying? How are we to understand situations where despite our deepest, most agonized prayers, the one for whom we pray dies? If prayer makes a difference, why doesn't it always make the difference of healing? And if prayer does indeed make a difference, does the death of the one for whom we have prayed mean that we simply did not pray enough—that if we had only given God more prayers to use for the well-being of this dear person, then the person would live? Is it our "fault" that he or she dies, through our neglect of prayer?

In working with these issues, I follow the fundamental dynamics already given. God works with the world as it is in order to lead it toward what it can be. Prayer changes the way the world is, and therefore changes what can be.

The application of these dynamics to prayers for healing requires recognition that mortality is part of the way the world is, and that immortality within the conditions of history is not part of our possibilities in the world. Prayer can make a difference to recovery when in fact an illness is not a "sickness unto death," or terminal, but prayer cannot eliminate our mortality. Each of us will encounter one disease or dysfunction that leads to our death.

Prayers for healing must take place in the full recognition of our mortality, since in one sense such prayers are a defiance of our mortality. We cry out that yes, we know quite well, thank you, that we are mortal, and that this loved one is mortal, but in *this* instance, Lord, override this mortality! Our own well-being is so interwoven with the well-being of this one that should he die, should she die, we would as well. Oh God, remove this unbearable mortality; let us live!

Over one hundred years ago there were many such godly prayers for healing. Not only all the persons for whom those prayers were made, but also all those who made them are now certainly dead. Do we say that God answered their prayers, God just said no? How superficial an answer! The fact is that the context for prayers of healing is our mortality. We will all die; it is not a question of if, but a question of when. The wonder is that given our fragility, and all the illnesses we contract, all but one of these illnesses are reversible. But it is a given that sooner or later we will each encounter the "sickness unto death," whether it comes through accident or through virus or through bacteria or simply through the fact that we will wear down, wear out, and die.

Too often prayers for healing are requested or offered as if the fact of our mortality were somehow a fable, or as if the norm of our mortality is that we should be in our nineties and die in our sleep. But how few people live to their nineties, or die quietly in the sleep of old age! The stark reality is that we encounter our mortality through all the spectrum of our years. In my own family, my grandfather died at 84, my father at 52, my mother at 70, my nephew at 25, my granddaughter but five-and-a-half months in the womb, and my son-in-law at 38. It is odd to think that somehow the norm, like the goal, is that we ought to die at 90 and in our sleep. Life and death are not so simply calculated.

So how and why do we pray for healing? Since we die anyhow, and it is simply a question of when, why not accept the reality and devote our prayers to other things? Would not God will it so? God wills the well-being of this world, even in the midst of its fragility and mortality, and not all illnesses need be terminal. Prayers for healing make a difference in what kinds of resources God can use as God faithfully touches us with impulses toward our good, given our condition. Those prayers can make the difference between reversing a not-yet-irreversible illness or not; therefore, God bids us to pray. But only God knows the point of that irreversibility, and in some diseases, it is with the very onset. For we creatures are, despite our toughness, most fragile.

God knows when irreversibility in any disease actually sets in. Prior to irreversibility, prayers give God more to work with in influencing a person, body and soul, to fight a particular disease. Think of it: did God decide that my son-in-law Butch, with a wife and three young children, should die? Was it God who afflicted Butch with myelocytic leukemia? Or is it not rather the case that in this finite world of fragility and interdependence it's a wonder we live as long as some of us do? Our bodies interact with many influences, both genetic and environmental, and mortality is built into the system for all creaturehood. The complexity of our embodiedness that provides us with the capacity for conscious participation in life is a fragile complexity, subject to breakdown. I do not know what disposes one person and not another to leukemia, save that our vulnerabilities are variable. But I do know that God works with us as we are to lead us to where we can be, with a preferential option toward deeper and richer communities of well-being. Surely God, and not simply Cathy, their children, and all who loved Butch, cared for his continued participation in this life. But when a disease such as leukemia is irreversible—and only God knows when—then not even God can make the ill one live—in this life. Prayers for healing are offered since we do not know the state of any disease. If reversibility is still possible, God can use our prayers to bring healing about.

But what if irreversibility is the case, what then? Shall we stop our prayers for healing? Of course not, for healing comes in many forms, and there is a health that is deeper than death. I saw it manifested in my own mother on her deathbed. We learned with a shock that my mother was dying. We flew to her, my brothers and I, from Costa Rica, San Francisco, Boston, and Pittsburgh. And when we arrived at the hospital in Dallas we were shocked when the elevator door opened at her floor, and we saw the dreaded word: *oncology*. We had been told only that something was wrong with her liver. Then we saw her swollen body, yellowed with the sickness that was indeed unto death. I prayed without ceasing during that hospital vigil, first pleading with God to save her, and then pleading with God to let her die swiftly to end her agony. In those first days of staying with my mother while the nurses bathed her, I noted the torn flesh on her poor belly where the adhesive had pulled away from the incision. The torn place was raw and oozing. And I prayed for her healing, and daily stayed by her as she was bathed, and to my mystification I watched that ugly sore heal. I confess it contributed to my anger: "God, you are healing this stupid sore, but it's not her sore that's the problem, it's her liver; why can't you do something about that?" But I learned that what forms of healing are possible are given, even in the sickness unto death. And her skin healed, while her urine turned black.

The forms of healing, I learned, are not only physical. At one point my mother, who had been in a semi-coma, roused herself and miraculously lifted her head and upper body from the bed, stretching out her arms toward us, her grown children. My brothers took her arms; I, at the foot of the bed, touched her feet. She looked at me and said a cryptic, "Do you want to join me? It's affirming." At first I inwardly cringed—to join her in death! No! But in the instant I knew she was right. We *had* each joined her, through our deep love and our prayers that so united us with her, and it *was* affirming. We were touching the profound places of the human spirit in that hospital room, and discovering that the process of dying was holy. Then she looked at us all and said, "My heart is filled with overwhelming love." I knew then that my prayers were answered, and my mother died a healthy woman. There is a health that is deeper than death.

And so it was with Butch. He joined a prayer group of women at his church, meeting each Tuesday to lift the needs of the church and the world to God in prayer. He who was prayed for joined in prayers for others. And so it should be. Prayer is that great and strange work that is our continuous privilege and responsibility, regardless of our condition. In the process of joining with the women in prayer, Butch grew even more deeply into the heart of that small Christian community, St. Christopher's Episcopal Church in Dallas. The congregation itself, interacting in the drama of Butch's struggle for life, grew even more closely knit. I remember the Sunday when Cathy had gone to the hospital to bring Butch home again, to wait for the next crisis. I had taken the children to church, and was sitting in their usual front row, and the eucharist was just about to be offered. I heard a sound from the congregation and turned to see Butch and Cathy coming haltingly down the aisle, Butch on his crutches. The children and I joined them at the communion rail as they led the congregation in taking bread and wine together. God works with the world as it is to lead it to where it can be, always—if we will follow—in the direction of deeper and richer modes of human community.

Butch died during the bone marrow transplant. A donor had been found, but too late. His weakened body could not survive the grueling process of the transplant. We softly sang the liturgy of the church he loved as he died—"surely, it is God who saves us; we will trust in God and not be afraid." Again I learned the holiness of death, even while also drinking deeply of its pain and grief. It is not good that Butch died—but it is very good that Butch lived. There is no doubt that it would be better if he continued to live out his life, being father to his growing children and husband to my daughter, contributing to the richness of his family, his community, and therefore to this world.

But though this did not happen, God used the many prayers for Butch's healing. They contributed to his buoyancy of spirit, to the endurance that he and Cathy and the children found in the strength of their own love, the love of their families, and the love of that little congregation daily poured out for them. Prayers for the terminally ill can work a health that is deeper than death. And underneath are the everlasting arms.

I learned in the months following Butch's death that prayers for healing have a continuing effect. We all grieved with Cathy and the children, and for ourselves as well.

And we continued in our prayers. On my visits to Dallas my growing grandchildren would throw themselves in my arms, covering me with hugs and kisses, and I would know that they were healing: a child who can still love openly, having suffered great loss, is a healthy child. And I watched my dear daughter live through her grief, with its rage and despair and aching emptiness. I rejoiced when a new job opportunity came along and I saw her rise to meet its challenge; I thanked God as I saw her reach out toward relationships. And I began to learn that the prayers for healing that could not be answered with Butch's recovery are now being answered through the health of his young family. The healing of Cathy, Garth, Graham, and Kent is the healing of Butch as well. For they have been "joined with him" in his death through their participation in his suffering, and I believe that by the resurrection power of God Butch is joined with them as they heal and open their own hearts to love and life. Healing comes in many forms, one of which is in the ability of the survivors to embrace life lovingly once again.

If indeed God receives the world in every moment, then God receives us in every moment. We certainly have no consciousness of ourselves "in God," for our consciousness is always newly created, oriented toward our living. Would it be so strange to think that upon death, when there is no newly created consciousness in the continuation of our histories, we might experience ourselves in God as participants in God's own life? And if such could happen, would it not be the case that as God experiences the continuing events of the world, we who are held in the life of God would also experience the continuing stories of earth? If so, then Butch experiences the recovery of Cathy and the boys, and their healing literally becomes his healing as well. It would also follow that, since God gives us guidance for each moment based upon who and where we are and also upon God's own resources, that Butch's life in God becomes part of the resources mediated to Cathy and the children as they pick up their lives again after Butch's death. God interacts faithfully with the world, giving to the world and receiving from the world, and death does not stop this interaction, it merely changes its form. There is a healing that is deeper than death.

These experiences of prayer in the context of terminal illness illustrate only one form of the effectiveness of prayers for healing. Prayers for healing, even when the illness in question is thought to be terminal, sometimes contribute to a reversal toward health for the one for whom we pray. In these happy cases, God can combine the divine resources with those of the person's own self and with the communities of personal and professional care surrounding the ill person. Recovery occurs, and those who prayed in agony pray in rejoicing gratitude for the renewed health of the one they love. God alone knows when such reversal is and is not possible in identified terminal cases. Thus, to give prayers for healing in the context of terminal illness is to pray for the health that is possible, whether that be total recovery, partial recovery, or the recovery of those who mourn. In releasing such prayers to God, we look for and rejoice in the forms of healing that can be and are given.

Because prayers for healing issue usually in recovery (for we survive all but one of our illnesses!) there is often the phenomenon of self-blame when in fact the illness of one we love issues into death. There seems to be some psychic movement of dealing with grief that takes us through this dark passage. If in fact our prayers make a difference to what God can do, and if in fact the one for whom we pray dies, do we then have a right to blame ourselves, and to say that if only we had prayed harder, or longer, or earlier, or more fervently, or more constantly, or more whatever, God could have saved him, her?

The phenomenon of self-blame happens often, regardless of whether it focuses upon how or whether one prayed. Perhaps it is rooted in our very interdependence, so that at some level we know we contribute to one another, sustain one another, with our own energy. When one we have loved with our very being fails, have we contributed less than enough? And so the questions and blaming perhaps arise from our deep sense of interdependence. But this very interdependence means that we do not and cannot exercise full control in our own or another's life. Other forces than our own also interact interdependently, for our good or for our ill, and control is never total; it is always shared.

Prayer is a partnership with God, not a manipulation of God. Prayer is prompted by God, and released to God. It is not our business to second-guess after the fact what could or would have happened had we done thus or so. We might as well blame God for not prompting us more forcefully to prayer, for does not God give us a guiding impulse in every moment of our being? Perhaps we prayed less than we did because God knew the condition of irreversibility, and did not prompt us to pray for recovery. All that we truly know is that, being mortal, our loved one had a sickness unto death. We release our prayers to God; we must release our loved one unto God as well. We are Christians, after all, and a people who live from and toward the God of resurrection power. God, not we, is the only one who really knows the might-have-beens of life.

The recourse to feelings of guilt and self-blame is prayer, naming before God all our feelings of failure and inadequacy in the honesty of who we are and how we are. Just as we are called to release our prayers of intercession to God, even so we are called to release our prayers of confession to God, and then to get on with it. We must trust this God unto whom we release our prayers, and look for the health that is deeper than death.

So, then, prayer that takes place in an interdependent world most surely involves prayers of intercession for healing, even for those who are terminally ill. Our praying makes a difference to what God can do. We offer our prayers for well-being, knowing that God will fill in the blanks of precisely what that well-being can be. And we know that there is no inadequacy in our praying, no matter how inadequate we might feel, for God's own self, through the Spirit, prompts our prayers, receives our prayers, and translates our prayers into the stuff for God's doing. And so we release our prayers to God to whom we give them, trusting this God who works with us all to do with them as God can and will.

In an interdependent, relational, contextual world, our praying constitutes a dance with God that makes a difference to what God can do in the world. For God works with the world as it is to lead it to what it can be. And prayer changes the way the world is, and therefore changes what is yet possible in the world. We can never predict in detail what that transformation will be, but since it comes from God, in interaction with this world, we do know this—in this world, it will be toward a finite form of resurrection, in a transformation that the world can bear. And who knows what it will be in that great resurrection which is yet before us, our resurrection into God's own life?

CHAPTER SIX

Prayers of Personal Confession

There are two major types of prayers of confession: personal and corporate. While the dynamics employed in both are similar, the situations differ enough to warrant separate treatment. Prayers of personal confession refer to naming ourselves before God as we truly are, owning to God and to ourselves the harm that we have done to others. The work of naming is at the same time the work of contrition and release toward the trans—formation that is yet possible for ourselves and others. Prayers of corporate confession deal with not so much the sins of each person, but the web of ill-being in which we together participate. Together we exploit the earth, we implicitly or explicitly tend toward fear or hatred of those whom we think too different from ourselves, and we subtly or openly despise the poor through actions that ensure their continued poverty. Together we engage in massive national egotisms that exploit weaker nations and engage in wars. Corporate confession supplements personal confession by drawing us before God to repent social sins that create ill-being in this world. Corporate and personal confession supplement each other, and both are always in order.

The most concise yet profound confession of sin is given in the Lord's Prayer. The petition is, "Forgive us our trespasses, as we forgive those who trespass against us." Alternatively, the word *debts* is used; in either case, the petition asks forgiveness for our violation of boundaries, our incurring of fault. Notice that the petition is both corporate and personal: forgive us for our sins, as we forgive those who sin against us. The plural is not simply because there are corporate as well as personal sins for which we share guilt. Rather, the plural indicates the universality of sin; it assumes that we have sinned against others, and others have sinned against us.

Usually we take it greatly amiss when others sin against us, and not nearly so amiss when we sin against others (for we always have our justifying rationales ready for ourselves). But the petition jolts us into the reality that in this finite, fragile world we will both sin and be sinned against. Our own prayer for forgiveness should be open to God's forgiveness of those who sin against us.

The petition takes us beyond mere openness for the other's forgiveness. The prayer suggests that we can be mediators of God's forgiveness to those who sin against us, opening ourselves to their well-being. For if God is open to their well-being, should not we be also? And is not their well-being actually our own?

The Lord's Prayer is a daily prayer, and thus assumes that we live each day in need of the forgiveness of God and forgiveness received from and extended to each other. Daily we name who we are before God; daily we are called to be open to the communal well-being to which God faithfully leads us. We are called daily to live from the confession and forgiveness of sins.

Particular issues in personal confession have to do with the familiar dynamics developed in earlier chapters. God works with us as we are toward our good. Prayer changes "how we are," and therefore opens us to God's gracious call toward deeper personal and communal good. Through personal confession we attempt to name who we are and how we are, and thus bring ourselves more into conformity with God's greater knowledge of us. This openness before God can then unblock us from the hindrances against our good, and open us for transformation toward well-being. Through confession, we can live from the power of forgiveness of sins toward our own good and the good of others. Confession, naming us as we are, opens us to God's leading toward what we might yet be. Thus prayers of confession are highly pragmatic, functioning to open us to God, ourselves, and others.

The sins that we confess are all variations on the theme of ill-being. We believe that God desires the good of the world, and that God woos the world toward deeper and richer modes of human community. Hindrances to this good are both personal and corporate. The world's very structure is one where there is a natural competition for goods. For example, life itself depends upon the destruction of other modes of life; we eat to live. We have an inherent need to destroy something so that it might be food for ourselves, whether it be from vegetable or animal species. No wonder we offer prayers of thanksgiving for our food; its purchase is the sacrifice of some form of life for the sustenance of our own! Because it is so natural to take other life for our daily food, we too easily justify the extension of such behavior as we shore up our defenses against life's fragility. We go beyond the simple need for sustenance, and look to destruction in the form of greed, domination, and/or rapaciousness to secure what we perceive to be our own good as opposed to the good of others.

Likewise, aggression is no stranger to us human beings. Aggression in itself can be good, prompting us not only toward survival, but toward development of ego-strength. It can help us to dare to do things that are good but nonetheless a bit frightening to us. In all probability, aggression has its root in the "fight or flight" instincts of all mammals, including ourselves; it may have played an important evolutionary function in our very survival.

Our aggression can be activated by perceived violations of our own space or our own good, sometimes rationally, sometimes irrationally. I myself am generally not considered by myself or others to be an overly aggressive person, but I feel my own aggressiveness in a certain traffic situation. When I drive home from the School of Theology at Claremont to Upland after work, there is a route that I have learned to avoid during rush hour. The narrowing of the road from two lanes to one occurs just before a traffic light, and during rush hour most of the drivers move in an orderly fashion out of the narrowing lane and into the other. But there are always those few who zoom past the waiting cars to cut into the line close to where it ends at the light, causing the other cars to wait that much longer for their turn to cross the intersection. I cannot begin to tell you of my indignation when one of these rude drivers cuts me off just as I think I am about to receive my turn! The annoyance is strong enough that I have found another route home, leaving my aggressive instincts dormant, at least over this cause! However civil we may be, our aggressive instincts are not far beneath our civility. Even in their tamed state, they are capable of being raised to rage, giving us the illusion that we have a right to wreak ill-being on whoever or whatever has interfered with what we consider to be our rights or our well-being.

These natural instincts to sustain ourselves and defend ourselves are not sinful, but they can easily turn into instruments whereby we contribute unnecessarily to the ill-being of others, and this is sin. Additionally, we protect ourselves not only physically, but psychically. We exist in the tense paradox that we are relational, and therefore require relations for the nurturing of our souls—yet the very openness that invites relation also makes us vulnerable, and sometimes we try to close ourselves off in protection. How fragile we are! Our greatest strength and our greatest weakness both exist in and through the vulnerability of relation.

In response to this tension we easily fall to sins against ourselves and others. We can work our own ill-being by a fearfulness that causes us to close ourselves off from others. We can deny others access to who we are, hoarding our own resources for ourselves. Alternatively, we can take advantage of the vulnerability of others, tearing down their own self-esteem, or violating them physically, or using them for what we perceive to be our own interests, heedless of their own. The variations on the ill-being of sin are endless, ranging from horrible violation of others to more subtle omissions that neglect the common good.

We are such creatures that it is probably not possible for us not to sin, given the fragility of human existence. We are interlocked with one another in interdependence, but we can respond to this interlocking as if it were a locked prison rather than an open invitation to community. In ways ingenious and infinite we have shored up our defenses against each other, even while ready to cut the other down as if this could build ourselves up. In the words of the ancient confession, we have indeed "done those things we ought not to have done, and left undone those things we ought to have done."

But God works with the world as it is to lead it to where it can be, toward the goal of richer, deeper modes of human community. Given our situation, the world is always a place of sin! We are a motley crew struggling individually for limited goods, even as we also struggle toward a community of mutual, communal well-being. Our struggle is an ambiguous mixture of sin and holiness, for seldom is it the case that our acts of sin have no good in them, or that our acts of goodness have no sin in them. We are mixed creatures, hungering after a purer good.

Because we do have a "thirst for righteousness," we often feel ambiguous about our own ambiguous mix of good and evil. Our easiest sin is to hide our sin from our own eyes; to own the good we often rightly see within ourselves, and to ignore the bad. Worse yet, we "baptize" the bad with justifying reasons that make poor actions seem good in our eyes—though they have worked ill-being for others. We hardly know ourselves.

But God works with us as we are to lead us toward what we can be. The difficulty, of course, is that when we don't own how we "are," we ourselves become a hindrance to God's leading. Suppose we really are grasping and greedy, but we think of ourselves as generous, justifying our greedy conduct by explaining to ourselves that it is for some greater good. God works with us as we really are. But who is God to address? If God fashions impulses for us as we really are—greedy parading as generous—we will not recognize God's call, for we do not recognize ourselves. If God instead addresses us as we think we are, giving us opportunities for generosity, we cannot take these opportunities without letting go of our greed. We become like the proverbial child with a clenched fist stuck in the cookie jar of ourselves, unable to let go and move into our own better future. We must let go of our greed, but as long as we do not even acknowledge it, we cannot let it go.

It is not much better if we have left off the pretense of generosity, and simply accept ourselves as greedy, preferring it so. Our chosen way of amassing what we can for ourselves blinds us to the true richness of another way of life. We see everything in terms of what it can do for us alone. In this case, the leading that God can give is stymied, for all transformative possibilities must begin with a judgment against one's own greed (and hence against one's own self). But we continuously reject this possibility.

The paradox, of course, is that in cases of greed the true richness of the self lies in the communal good, for who we are is developed in interaction with the community. In a relational world, one's own spiritual richness is mediated through the richness of others, so that the good of the community is necessary to one's own good. But in my illustration, the greedy self sees richness not as something to be shared, but as a something to be hoarded. Paradoxically, the increase in material wealth is at the same time a decrease in spiritual health.

What can even God do? Impulses toward confession are God's way of leading one past the block of one's sin toward a richer and deeper self lived within communal interdependence. Thus confession, which is the contrite naming of who we really are, unblocks us, opening us up for our good. Naming is important, because honesty before God brings us into greater conformity with God's knowledge of us. Contrition is important, because unless we can name the ill quality with some sense that it is in fact an "ill" quality, we will not be ready to let it go in favor of the transformation God can make possible for us. Apart from this contrite naming, God is forced to address us again and again with the same baby-step possibility for transformation. There is no transformative future for a false self until it leaves off its falseness. So in a world where God works with us as we are, there is only one pathway toward richness of communal well-being, and that is honesty of spirit. God's leading toward confession is God's invitation to transformation.

In a process world our character is built up through habituated responses to God and others. We are dynamic creatures, and each of us at some time or other acts in ways that work ill for others. Each such action paves the way for its own repetition, and we can become so used to our acts of ill will that we no longer notice them. Confession opens us to self-knowledge, and therefore toward our greater communal good.

There are other dynamics involved in confession that draw on the sense of "meeting in God" that I developed in the chapter on intercession. I can illustrate this best through an account from my own experience. There was a time when I considered that my friend Nancy had wronged me. I remember being outraged at the nature of her "crime" and the failure of friendship. How I railed at her untrustworthiness and falsehood! Naturally, I considered her breach of trust to be wholly her fault. I loved my friend, but I confess that during this period I felt hatred for her, which is, of course, the other side of love. I wished that she would feel at least half the pain she had caused me—or twice as much! No, three times would be too good for her—I really was most wretched, without an ounce of charity. But I am a process theologian, and was teaching a summer class in process theology at the time. I remember walking across the campus, internally muttering imprecations against my hapless friend. The moment will always remain with me: suddenly I was stopped short, under a great shade tree. I just stood there, realizing with an awful awareness that if my theology has any adequacy at all, then

God had to be experiencing all the ill will I was so furiously directing toward my friend! All the hatefulness I directed toward her, God had to receive as well. Furthermore, in a relational world, Nancy was also being affected by my deep ill will toward her. In working with Nancy toward her good, God would have to cope with the ill will I was contributing to her. I was hindering the goodness of God! Furthermore, we "meet" in God—God receives Nancy in every moment of her living, just as God receives me, and in that holy meeting she was experiencing all my ill will, which indeed fulfilled my evil wishes. My ill will was thrice that which she had directed at me. I was overcome with contrition, and answered the call of God by confessing my sin against God and against Nancy. Through confession, I became open to the reconciliation that then occurred between me and Nancy, who was— and is—truly my friend.

Note that I had to confess sin against God as well as against Nancy and, indeed, against myself. If the language can be appropriately used, I can say that in hurting Nancy, I also "hurt" God. Even though God's own resources are such that the hurt given to God cannot destroy God (as it could Nancy), God nonetheless had to experience all my ill will. And such cannot be good, not even for God. In a world where God feels the world, all acts or intentions that work pain in the world work pain in God as well. Therefore, all sins against the world are also sins against God. Confession of sin must recognize this through the double confession: we have sinned against others, and in so doing, have sinned also against God.

What I learned through this episode is how peculiarly we are joined to each other through ill-being. Just as there is a union created through love, there is also a kind of shadow-union created through hatred. Union through love enriches, but union through hate fragments and impover-

ishes us. Our very hatred of the other ties our perceived
well-being to their ill-being; we are thus bound to them
not for good, but for ill. Such a parody of love's union
blocks us from our good; it is a union created as sin is
answered by further sin. In a relational world it is a union
that is a sorrow to God as well as to ourselves. Confession
of sin changes the nature of this union from ill-being to
well-being. It opens us for transformation.

Sin has a rippling effect, creating ill-being that spills
over beyond what may have been its intended sphere.
Though we confess our sin against another, we can never
know the full effect of our sin, either in the person we
have directly harmed, or in those who may have been
harmed secondarily. While the hurt to these others may be
secondary as far as we are concerned, it is primary from
their own perspective, and we share part of the blame. To
injure another is to know that others, who depend on that
other, will also be injured, and these others can, in their
own turn, perpetuate the pain. Thus, when we confess our
sins to God, we do so knowing that we do not have knowledge of the full extent of our sins. Confession therefore
requires not only a naming of what we know, but acknowledgment that there is a wider sphere of injury known to
God. Given this extensiveness to sin and its effects, confession must lead also to intercession, praying for the well-
being of those who suffer through our sins.

Our sins block us from receiving our own good. It is
not that God withholds good from us as our just punishment, for indeed, God also feels our suffering. Sin is
against God's good as well as against our own. The hardship
entailed by sin, whether it is like the misery I knew in my
alienation from my friend or the impoverishment of character that results from habitual sins like greed, is the suffering sin causes. It is not that first there is sin, and then
punishment: the sin is itself punishing. Confession does

not therefore take place in order to be followed by a period of punishment. To the contrary, confession clears the way for the suffering to stop. However, when confession is but the beginning of turning from sin, or when the effects of our sins have caused great harm not easily healed, then confession only begins the process of healing the suffering.

God's forgiveness does not wait for all the effects of our sin to disappear, any more than God's leading toward transformation waits. Rather, through confession God's will toward our well-being is immediately released. God's will toward our good is ever-present, but our sin blocks our ability to receive this good. Sin is like the dam that holds back the waters of God's grace; confession is like the breaking of the dam, releasing the divine waters for our thirsty souls. This divine will toward our well-being is itself God's forgiveness. Our reception of this forgiveness is at once our movement beyond our sin and into the transformation God makes possible for us.

Our Christian tradition speaks of the "unconditional forgiveness" God makes available to us in Christ. The ground of this forgiveness is not our own confession, or our own character, but God's own character as revealed to us in Christ. Through Christ, we learn to trust this God who is for us, and to dare the confessions that open us to God's well-being. God is ever open to our good, prompting us toward those prayers of confession that will open us, also, to the good of God. This is the grace of God, working toward us and for us, in the forgiveness of sins.

Confession is conversion. The call of God to confessional prayer is not like some means to another end, it is both means and end. Thus the process of confessing our sins is also the reality of experiencing the forgiveness of sins. We do not first confess, and then receive forgiveness—to the contrary, the confession is itself the appropriation of God's generous love, already long since manifest for us, toward us, in Christ. Nor is it the case that by confessing we thereby earn forgiveness—again, it is that the very act of confessing is the grace-laden act of appropriating that forgiveness. Confession is conversion; it is the *modus operandi* of living from the forgiveness of sin.

Prayers of confession are both momentary and continuous. In a momentary way, we name ourselves before God, bringing ourselves into conformity with the divine knowledge and the divine judgment, as much as is possible for us. But in a continuous way, we are called to live our confession. The openness to God's will for our well-being in community becomes our power to break from the sins we have named. When in fact our sins have deformed our characters, bending us far from God's will, our transformation may take considerable time. The forgiveness is immediate, depending on God's own character; the transformation may be slow, depending on our own character. Transformation is in fact the changing of our character. Thus we are called to live from the confession and forgiveness of sins as an event spanning our lives, rather than as an event interrupting our lives.

Prayers of confession are also prayers of thanksgiving for forgiveness, for confession and forgiveness are two sides of the same event. This is so because confession is what is called "performative" language—it is not different from the act to which it refers; it constitutes that act. For example, to say "I invite you" is itself the invitation; the words are the deed. Even so, by the grace of God, to confess is to be released from the sin that blocks us from God's transformative grace toward us. Confession opens us to the well-being of God. And to be open to the well-being of God is to be filled with gratitude that God receives us sinners, even in the full knowledge of who we are. God works with us as we are—and through our confession, leads us to where we yet can be. Thanks be to God.

CHAPTER SEVEN

Prayers of Corporate Confession

*O*ur sins are social as well as personal. If God calls us to communities of well-being, then all aspects of our social existence that work against well-being violate the call of God. This is sin. But while we are often quite aware of individual sins, we are often oblivious to corporate sins. This is not so surprising, since such sins can be so woven into the "way things are" that we assume they represent the way things ought to be.

Certain results follow from our unacknowledged participation in social sin: isolation, fragmentation, and powerlessness. I write as a middle-class woman, and we who are middle-class Americans fall easily into the illusion that we are separated from major social problems such as poverty, violence, and ecological destruction. We consider ourselves isolated from the immediate threat of such things. Indeed, many of us could ignore them if it were not for the shad-

ows they cast through their inevitable reiteration in the
evening news, and their occasional and fearful irruption
into our lives through crime. By and large, however, we
see the problems as outside ourselves.

But this very isolation fragments our social being, di-
viding us into strata of privilege and poverty. Pretending
to an isolation from the problems, we contribute to the
fragmentation of society. We make of society an uncom-
fortable collection of ethnicities, parties, and coteries
grouped loosely around one theme or another. This fragmentation, in turn, contributes to powerlessness, for
through fragmentation we perpetuate the problem rather
than participate in forms of resolution. When we read or
see the news of crime and corruption, we disown responsibility from the problems and therefore dissociate from any
claim that we ought to address the problems.

After all, how can I, an individual living in a suburb,
have any effect upon the rising homicide rate in the city?
How can I, a mere individual, affect the issues that place
nations in warring postures? What can I do about the
pervasive "isms" in our society that single out some for ill-
treatment? And how on earth can I address issues of
organized crime, or economic structures that ensure poverty and homelessness for so many? Whatever the issue
may be that drains well-being from society, the only clarity
about it is that it is too big for me, and I have neither the
power—nor the will—to address it. Powerlessness becomes
apathy, and I do nothing to engage the structures of evil
in society. And while I on occasion might feel a qualm of
dis-ease that I enjoy the comforts of my life while others
experience more directly the agonies of evil, the qualm
dispels as I creep back into my private myth of my own
innocence of these ills. I did not cause these problems;
why or how should I be held to account for addressing
them? There is a power in powerlessness, for it frees us

from responsibility and sends us back to the easier world of our own lives, and our own more manageable problems.

But as participants in society we are formed by the structures and values of society, be they for good or for ill—and usually they are a mixture of both. We imbibe these structures and values into our lives, perpetuating them for the next generation. We are Adam; we are Eve. We are responsible. And within the heart of our Christian faith there exists a resource of first resort that can cut through our isolation, our fragmentation, our powerlessness. That resource is corporate prayers of confession in the church.

The tragedy of a church that confesses only its faith, and not its sin, is that if it cannot confess its corporate sin, how can it truly confess faith? Faith lives from the forgiveness of sins, or it does not live at all. A Christianity that is cut off from its acknowledgment of its own participation in sin and need of forgiveness is like a plant cut off from its roots, and it will wither. Without the church's confession of sin, God's most powerful force for social renewal is left immobilized, locked away in a spiral of individualism that addresses only individual problems and ignores the social dimensions of all personal sins.

In our penchant for individualism, we privatize the Christ as well as sin. We confess neither publicly nor corporately; rather, we confess to God privately the various personal sins that we have done through commission or omission. We thus confess the mote and ignore the log. But individual confession alone is not adequate in regard to social sin.

There is a pervasive commonality in the warp and woof of society; we're in the soup together, and it takes all of us together to create the demons that afflict us. It also takes all of us together to name the demons. We participate in corporate problems that require corporate confession. By failing to confess sin corporately, we do not avail ourselves of the power of confession, which is corporate renewal and resurrection power for the transformation of the structures of oppression that we now confess.

What exactly is the corporate confession of sin, and what is its power? The power of corporate confession is the triple identity that it works, and the sense in which that triple identity overcomes isolation, fragmentation, and powerlessness. If passive participation in social sin is like a union that isolates, fragments, and destroys, confession becomes the antidote with its own power toward a union that draws together into community. Such a community has the potential of being used by God to transform social structures from ill-being toward well-being. Individually we may be able to do little against social ills, but corporately and in the power of God, we can do much.

The first aspect of our identity is an identification with the problem on the personal level. This leads to personal confession, but also to confession with the community of faith in recognition of our communal identity. Finally, it leads to identification with God's own will toward communal well-being.

The movement into corporate confession can begin with personal realization of one's participation in corporate sin. Unacknowledged sin is not absent sin, it is simply disguised sin. An example may clarify my meaning. Years ago, when I was a young woman of twenty, I worked as a secretary in a small Boston office. One of my coworkers was an African-American woman, and we often went to lunch together, sometimes joined by many of her friends who worked in nearby offices. I wondered sometimes as we walked together in a group, with myself the only Euro-American, why I felt awkward.

And then it happened that I had an opportunity to take my very first trip from New England to the South. When I arrived at the airport I headed for the rest room, and saw two—one with a sign reading "colored," and the other plain. I thought perhaps the sign signified that the one had just been freshly painted, and so used the other. But during the weekend I learned what the sign meant, and when I returned to Boston on Monday I looked at my office friend with new eyes that reflected shame and confusion. Our times of having lunch together began to dwindle, for I was embarrassed by my new knowledge, though I never verbalized why.

Now, many years later, I reflect differently about my awkwardness and my embarrassment. I was a participant in the problem, and not simply an observer of the problem. I had already imbibed the structures of racism into my living—I, too, was racist, despite my unconsciousness of the fact. I experienced the personal results of my unacknowledged racism—awkwardness and shame—but did not possess the tools to trace these feelings to their roots. To that extent, I remained separated in consciousness not only from the problem, but from the fullness of myself. Now, years later, I know the roots of those feelings— and now, years later, I have a better knowledge of myself.

Confession holds within it all those dynamics—it has the power of naming the problem and the self, it has the power of bringing to consciousness a deeper knowledge of who we really are. And insofar as confession through its naming unites us with the problem and ourselves, it overcomes the debilitation of our false isolation from the problem, opening us up to modes of redress. Insofar as it deepens our own sense of self-identity, it also means that through that deeper self-knowledge, there is literally more of who we are to be utilized in dealing with the problem.

I have used racism as an illustration, but one could just as well go down the list of social ills of our day and trace the lines of participation—naming the sins is naming ourselves, and therefore appropriating more of our true being for the responsible work of living. Therefore, the first mode of identity accomplished in confession deepens our self-understanding, enlarging our awareness of who we really are. Social sin is not something outside us, it is part of the warp and woof through which we have woven ourselves; it has entered, in our own personalized way, into our identities. The message of sin is that it taints the very character it forms, so that walking away from it is no easy task—it requires walking away from ourselves! But in confession, we shed the myth of innocence, and dare by the power of God to name the reality. I don't mean that we wallow in it—that serves nothing. But we require a sober recognition of who we really are. To say that we must name the problem is to say that we must name ourselves. Unnamed, sin continues to exercise its effects. Naming it, we begin to transcend it, to switch the basis of control.

The second mode of identity that results from naming our participation in social sins is a new and deeper identification with one another in the confessing community. The very nature of social sin is that it is a shared problem, a common affliction and a common struggle. There is a power in this identification with one another as community, particularly given the peculiarities of the confession of sin.

Perhaps you have seen it develop, as I have, in a workshop dealing with some social issue—often racism, but also issues of sexism, or classism, or heterosexism, or handicappism, or any of the dreary list of "isms" that drain us through the taint of social sin. These workshops, designed to raise consciousness, are never easy—certainly, one would rather be almost anywhere else. The responses from these workshops are predictable, and reflect our ignorance of the working of social sin. Failing to see sin's corporate as well as personal nature, we respond first of all simply on the personal level with what could be called, "guilt-trip-itis." There is anger at the thought that we are accused, but the very anger has a double edge. It is directed at the ones responsible for the workshop, but also at the uneasiness within ourselves. And it is this latter uneasiness that develops into guilt-trip-itis. This phenomenon is simply the illusion that the purpose of confession is to lay guilt trips upon whatever dominant group is being addressed, as if guilt-tripping is the purpose of the whole experience.

Yet if we stay with that anger at imposed guilt, accepting it as a stage and moving through it and beyond it, we begin to discover the positive power of communal confession for corporate identity. The issue is that every social sin is a communal problem, and *therefore* it is an individual problem. We are in it together, and to name this corporate center of the problem is a source of power.

I can illustrate this power in an easier sense by using a less tension-racked mode than sin. When my mother died she endured the agony of thirteen days of barely mitigated pain. We, her children, felt pain in our own beings as well when we saw her suffering. But through that whole time I felt the support of those who loved us, who prayed for us; it was sometimes as if the whole church were present in that room, bearing the pain with us. Did it alleviate the pain? The answer is an odd yes and no—the pain continued, there was no way out of it, only through it. But it was like holding a ten-ton boulder, and then realizing that there were many others bearing it alongside us. The comfort of their identity with us in the pain was the strength to endure.

Even so, when we take corporate confession seriously, and identify with one another as participants in the problem of social sin, there is a bearing together of a pain too great for any one of us. Through confession there can come about a new sensitivity to one another, a new understanding of one another, a new strengthening through one another. The corporate prayer of confession turns the bond of isolated individualistic iniquity into the weaving of togetherness, into the world of "bear ye one another's burdens, and so fulfill the law of Christ." Just as there can be a form of power over social sin in our naming of and identification with the problem, even so there is the possibility of transcendence over the isolation of social sin through the identity with one another that comes about through confession.

The third mode of identity accomplished in the corporate prayer of confession is the deepest of all, and the one that makes the others possible. This is the identification with the God to whom we pray. Central to our faith is the confession that God identifies with us in our sin through Christ, and that Christ died not simply for the individual, but for the world. We might even be able to say that we know Christ died and rose for us because Christ died and rose for the world, and we are part of the world. It is a corporate love manifested by God in Christ—not to the annihilation of the individual, but strangely and paradoxically, for the true identity of the individual, who after all is an individual in and through the community. God identifies with us in our sin—and therefore, wonder of wonders, allows the possibility of our identification with God.

The prayer of confession is addressed not to one another, but to God, and becomes our own identification with the God who identifies with us. And if we gain a measure of transcending power through our identification with the problem, and if we also gain a measure of transcending power through our identification with one another, then imagine the power now not simply of transcendence, but of resurrection, that is made available to us through the double identification of God with us, and us with God.

This last form of identity in fact undergirds the first two. The problem with sin is that it isn't exactly an easy thing to confess. We think of ourselves—usually—in fairly livable terms. Many of us actually like who we are. We strive for good self-images, and suffer without them. Naming our complicity in evil challenges those comfortable self-images, and looking with any depth at all into the character of the evil would undo us. How do we have the strength for such confession? It's a little like the pitiable person who feels a lump where it should not be, but does not seek a doctor's opinion for fear of what that opinion might be. We cannot bear the knowledge, so we shrink from it. Even so with the odiousness of sin, tainting our natures. How would we have the strength to bear such a full knowledge of ourselves and our communities?

The answer, of course, is that God already has a full knowledge of who we are, but offers us love nonetheless. We confess to God—and God can bear our confession. Therefore, so can we. The identification with God, who holds our identity within the fullness of God's own knowledge and love, empowers us for the work of confession, and its corollary deeper naming of ourselves.

And likewise with one another. It is in the context of prayer that we name our togetherness, confessing who we are, stumbling and fumbling with the words. Each of us, relating to God, is empowered for our mutual relations with one another. God holds you, as God holds me, so God holds us—*we* are held together in the God who so fully knows us! The bond that unites us is our mutual participation in God, therefore enabling this prayer. God is the God of the community, and *therefore* of the individual. Because of our mutual identification with God, we are identified anew with one another.

So the prayer of corporate confession carries a triple identity within it, which by the grace and call of God gives the church the power to become a force against sin both within itself and in the larger society, for the purpose of confession is to release the power of forgiveness. Forgiveness, in turn, is the power to redress to whatever extent possible the wrong. The confessing church lives its confession in and through its daring to become a force for good. Because of its confession, it no longer stands aside from social ills—it knows that it itself has helped to perpetuate those ills. In the power of forgiveness it continuously opens itself to God's transforming power within its own structures, and continuously looks for ways God might use the communal force of the church to redress the same sins within its larger society. The church that has learned how to criticize itself and to name itself before God is a church that God can use to criticize society toward its own social transformation. Social ill is met by social good.

Thus the church is called to confess not only its faith, but also its participation in the social sins of each age. Through its corporate confession comes the power to be united with the resurrection power of God. In place of the isolation, fragmentation, and powerlessness of complicity in social evils, there is union with ourselves, one another, and God. This union becomes a new resource for the continuous work of transforming the structures of sin into structures of communal well-being.

The final point is that corporate confession, like personal confession, reinforces this need for the continuing process of confession, forgiveness, and transformation. The church does not offer its corporate prayer of confession one Sunday, and then assume the issue is over and done with. The tentacles of sin require more than that. In a sense, alcoholism gives the best illustration: a recovering alcoholic is a recovering *alcoholic*. The nature is still there; its manifestation is transformed. In a similar way, we have been formed through social structures that deform us, individually and corporately. The very transformations made possible through confession retain in some fashion the lingering reality of that which called for transformation in the first place. And when we as a church work corporately toward society's transformation from these same sins, we do so as those who continuously experience the struggles and transformations firsthand. We are recovering sinners—always "standing in the need of prayer." We live continuously from the forgiveness of sins—and therefore we live continuously from the confession of sins.

Confession of sin is not easy—bluntly, real confessions we do not like; they are troubling. But I am convinced that given our involvement in the tentacles of sin, existing within us as absorbed structures of the "way of things" that work toward ill-being, we must be a confessing church, entering into the conversion process whereby there is hope that we might ourselves be transformed, and therefore be an ongoing force for the transformation of society. For the purpose of confession, of course, is precisely that: transformation. It is the peculiarity of Christian faith that we dare to name powers of destruction precisely because we are convinced that there is a greater power for transformation. Through corporate confession we ourselves are graciously empowered to dare to enter into the resurrection power of God, becoming for the world around us a community that mediates redemption in the midst of the problem of sin.

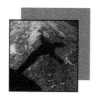

CHAPTER EIGHT

Liturgical Prayers

The unity of the church is woven in and through the threads of its prayers, like a great tapestry of our togetherness before and in God. I have long been struck by the prayer of Jesus recorded in John 17, where Jesus prays that those who follow him shall be one, even as he and God are one. The deepest form of unity between Jesus and God evident in this chapter is the very prayer itself: the sharing is intimate and impassioned on the eve of the crucifixion, and we ourselves are drawn into this union through Jesus' intercession for us. We continue in that union through our own prayers, which are like extensions of that prayer in Gethsemane. Insofar as we participate in that prayer-filled union, generation after generation, we become God's answer to Jesus' own prayer.

There is some irony in the fact that we as a church have looked not to our prayer life as an answer to Jesus'

prayer for our unity, but to our thought life. We have somehow thought that we most deeply show our unity by a
singular conformity of thought. But how can we all think
alike? Doctrinal diversity has been the single most common characteristic of the church through all its long history! We have not dealt well with this diversity, for we have
not understood that human thinking is conditioned and
hence variable, as was indicated in Chapter 1. Thus we
tended to respond to the diversity with concern at best
and hatred at worst, thinking that those who disagreed
with us were by definition not in unity with us, and therefore not in unity with Christ. Tragically, we as a church
have been many "we's," creating contentious factions, each
of which deems all the others heretical—for if "we" are
right, and if doctrinal conformity is necessary as an answer
to Jesus' prayer for unity, then are not all the others wrong?
And so we have tended to set up our own thinking as the
norm for Christian unity. But if doctrinal uniformity is
the unity for which Jesus prayed, then God has been sin-
gularly unsuccessful in answering Jesus' prayer.

But if prayer is the unity! Throughout John 17, Jesus
is shown to us in the depths of communion with God in a
prayer of intercession for us. He asks not that we know
doctrine, but that we know God, that we may be protected,
that we may be one, and that the love of God shall be in
us. Unifying these requests is the medium through which
they are uttered: prayer itself. Jesus is one with God in
prayer. Might it not be that our own praying is in fact the
living fulfillment of Jesus' prayer? In prayer we know God;
through prayer we deepen our openness to God's protec-
tive guidance; through prayer we become more receptive
to God's love in us; through prayer we are made one with
God in Christ, and with each other in Christ. This kind of
unity is peculiarly present in liturgical prayer. In the liturgy
of the church we join ourselves with all those Christians

who preceded us, and we provide the transitional link for all those who will come after us.

Liturgical prayers embrace the entirety of the church's worship, from invocation to benediction. They may take the form of a brief collective address to God, a hymn or psalm, or responsive prayers between liturgist and people, such as during celebration of the Lord's Supper. These prayers may be very formal, as presented in a prayer book, or they may be informal in a way that is unique to a particular congregation. But whether formal or informal, liturgical prayers are the people's worship, lifting the entire service as an offering to God.

While there are differences in the particular ways a congregation participates in liturgical prayers, there are nonetheless deep commonalities. Liturgical prayers not only present the church's worship to God, these prayers also mark the various traditions within the Christian church. Within the Western church, Roman Catholic, Lutheran, and Episcopalian churches all follow a similar liturgical pattern. Churches in the Reformed tradition likewise manifest a similar order, as do the "free" churches, such as Baptist. Some traditions, such as Methodist, can reflect either the Anglicanism of John Wesley or the free churches of the American frontier. In all these varieties of liturgical prayer, the commonality is their uniform address to God, and the sense in which each type inherits from a common past. No matter how various the forms of liturgy within a church, they trace their lineage through the centuries of the Christian tradition to its origins in the New Testament church and in Judaism.

The book of Acts recounts the fact that the disciples regularly went to the synagogue or the temple in Jerusalem to pray. Christian prayer is rooted in early Jewish forms of prayer, which themselves followed a liturgical form. They typically began with either the blessing of God or a direct thanksgiving to God. This opening of the prayer could be in either the second or third person. The prayers of the book of Psalms provide an example, for there the form of address to God moves easily between second and third person, often within a single psalm. The prayer that is Psalm 145, for example, begins "I will extol you, my God and King, and bless your name forever and ever. . . . Great is the LORD, and greatly to be praised. . . ." The "great is the LORD" is as much a prayer as is "I will extol you." It is as if the prayer given to God in the company of the faithful included holy conversation. Praying was not a solitary act, but a communal act, and therefore included the praise of God spoken to one another as well as the praise of God spoken directly to God. Prayer was the lifting of the community to God in praise, whether this praise addressed God as "you" or as "the Lord."

Following the blessing or thanksgiving to God, Jewish prayer typically named the basis for the blessing or thanksgiving in God's mighty works. This could be a recounting of God's saving acts in Exodus or in the Jewish return from exile, or simply God's preserving work in bringing forth daily blessings. Often both historic and contemporary reasons were named. This recounting of God's acts was often accompanied by extensive praise of God. Following this, the prayers moved into petitions and intercessions, which were the main body of the prayer. These concluded with the expressed hope that the petitions conformed to God's will or served God's glory. Then the prayer was brought to a close by returning once again to the blessing of God in praise for God's eternal glory.

It was not unusual within Judaism for subgroups to insert their own forms of prayer into the petition section of the liturgy. This unique form of praying became a mark of the group's identity within the larger Jewish community. Our most notable example of this is Jesus' response to the disciples' request to teach them to pray. The version recorded in Luke 11 appears to end abruptly with the petition, "And do not bring us to the time of trial," but this would not have been the ending at all for Jesus or the disciples. Rather, it signaled the resumption of the general prayer. The writer of Matthew's version indicated this by adding the final praise of God in "for the kingdom and the power and the glory are yours forever. Amen."

To summarize, Jewish prayers at the time of Jesus followed a formula of first praising God; second, naming the reasons for that praise in the communal experience of God in history; third, voicing petitions and intercessions (including the unique forms of these as developed within various subgroups of Judaism); fourth, stating the conformity of the petitions with God's will; and finally, returning to the praise of God. This liturgy formed the worship life of Jesus and his followers, and became the pattern for early Christian prayer.

As the early Christians adapted the Jewish form of prayer into their own emerging distinctiveness, their major difference rested in the part of the prayer that recounts the ground of prayer. For Christians, the mighty work of God became named as God's work for us in Jesus Christ. This is apparent in the prayers that often begin the epistles, such as Ephesians 1:3, "Blessed be the God and Father of our Lord Jesus Christ, who has blessed us in Christ with every spiritual blessing in the heavenly places," or Galatians 1:3, "Grace to you and peace from God our Father and the Lord Jesus Christ, who gave himself for our sins to set us free from the present evil age, according to the will of our God . . . to whom be the glory forever and ever. Amen." Also, Christian prayers typically opened with thanksgiving rather than blessing, although the example in Ephesians is a notable exception. Thus the typical Christian form of liturgical prayer was first thanksgiving and praise to God;

second, the ground of that praise in the work of God in Christ; third, daily petitions and intercessions, culminating with the Lord's Prayer; fourth, the conformity of the prayer with the will of God as revealed in Christ (". . . .in Jesus' name"); and finally, a return to praise and thanksgiving to God.

The early church followed the Jewish practice of praying at least three times daily in the morning, noon, and evening; a fourth period of prayer was also often set for midnight. While it was customary to go to the house of worship for daily prayer, it was also acceptable to pray at the appointed hour in one's home or workplace or even on the street (as was obvious in the parable of the pharisee and the publican). Prayers said privately, however, were considered part of the corporate praying of the church. Again, prayers were a communal activity, so that whether one prayed privately or in a congregation, prayers were the work of the church as a whole, and were understood as such.

The Christian form of prayer was to face east either standing or kneeling, with arms raised and eyes looking upward. The importance of facing east had to do with the fact that Christian prayer uniformly looked toward the coming of God's kingdom. By praying in Christ's name, the church understood itself to be participating in bringing the reign of God into human history. The expectation was that Christ would return from the east, so that by facing east during prayer the church was expressing its anticipation of Christ's coming.

In addition to the daily prayers, services were held three times a week—Wednesday, Friday, and Sunday—in a designated house of worship. Wednesday and Friday were most likely services of the word, where prayer was accompanied with hymns, psalms, and readings. These readings were from prophetic aspects of the Old Testament and from the emerging Christian writings. The Sunday worship culminated in the ritual of the Lord's Supper and a community meal. The liturgy of the Lord's Supper generally followed the pattern of prayer given above, with the actual sharing in the bread and the wine taking place in the midst of the liturgical prayer.

Even all these centuries later, we can recognize some of our own practices in the customs of those first Christians. We no longer face east (although for centuries it continued as the practice of the church), and we may not be quite so conscious that our prayers are part of the coming of God's reign, but the Sunday service of the word today, as then, includes hymns, psalms, readings, and often the Lord's Supper, and the framework that holds these parts together is still the embracing act of prayer.

In Protestant worship we often see the sermon as the major point of the service, but I suggest that prayer is the major point of every service of worship, and that the whole service, including the sermon, be interpreted as extended prayer. For example, we often begin our services with invocations. Surely, we are not invoking God to be present among us; God is always present among us, and needs no such invocation. Rather, we invoke ourselves to be present to God, to lift our minds from our daily concerns to openness to God. Our hymns of praise are the liturgical recognition of our love to God; the union of our blended voices calls us to a union of blended hearts. These songs often recite the work of God for us in Christ, or the church's theological expression of the ground of God's work in the very nature of God. As such, the opening hymn of praise is analogous to the role of praise in the early church's liturgy of prayer.

Prayers of confession follow praise. Here we as a corporate body, united with one another in Christ, open our corporate identity to God and one another. Confession

opens us to our shared responsibility and our shared calling. It follows naturally from the praise of God—not to
emphasize our own contrasted lowliness, but because
through the praise of God, we recognize our high calling
to live as God's image. Confession not only names us as
we are; it names us as we can be, and hence confession
calls us to mission. Thus confession rightly follows the
praise of God in our liturgical worship together. Since confession also opens us to forgiveness, as noted in earlier chapters, the prayers of confession are also prayers of cleansing,
and of openness to God's fresh call.

And so we hear the text, prayerfully, as a cleansed
people, open now to hear God's corporate word. The word
is addressed to us most fundamentally at the corporate level,
for we are Christians not individually, but in the
togetherness created through our baptism into Christ.
While each of us has individually been baptized into Christ,
through that very baptism we are made members of one
another. We are *always* members of one another, whether
we are together or apart. But during the worship service
we are uniquely expressing our togetherness, and so the
hearing of the word at the service is first and foremost
addressed to us as a congregation, as a people. The word
recounts God's grace and God's works for us. The
faithfulness of God experienced by God's people in the
past is the same faithfulness given to us today. Thus we
hear the word of God's faithfulness prayerfully, open to
God's continuous call.

The sermon offers opportunity for the application of
the text to us in our communal life together. As such, the
sermon is of a piece with the reading of the text. The one
who preaches shares with all of us the sermon the preacher
received in the study of the text, and this, too, we receive
prayerfully. The sermon may be instructive, and so guide
us in the deepening knowledge of God; it may be critical,

lifting up again some of those aspects of our earlier confession in order that we may be open to our own transformation. The sermon may be comforting, speaking God's grace to us in times of trial, or the sermon may be directive, suggesting specific ways that we as a people shall live out our calling. But whichever form the sermon takes, its giving and its receiving is in the context of worship, not a classroom. Thus the sermon must be bathed in prayer, which is openness to God's own guidance. This is so for the preacher and for the receivers of this word, for only in the context of prayer's openness to God can this sermon be used most effectively by God to shape and form the congregation.

For this reason, the prayers of the people best follow the word of the text and the sermon. Having joined in the praise of God, and openness to God through confession and through the word, the congregation is ready for the high point of the service, which is prayers of petition and intercession. God works with the world as it is to bring it to where it can be; prayers change the way the world is, and therefore change what can be. The congregation must bring its concerns to God: personal concerns for daily living, and corporate concerns for the church's mission. This includes prayers for the support and strength in righteousness of the leaders of the secular and religious community. But most importantly, the petitions and intercessions need to lift up the specific forms of mission given to this particular congregation. This mission will almost always involve Christian nurture, whether through the care exercised toward one another generally and in times of need, or in the formal educational work within the congregation.

Also, in some form or other, the church's mission is to live out the injunctions of Matthew 25, where Jesus identifies with the poor, the hungry, the thirsty, the imprisoned, and the sick. In small congregations, the focus may be on one form of need or the other, and in large congregations it may be that all forms are embraced within the church's mission. The church will be dealing with the issues on a social, political, or personal level—often, on all three. But unless the church is answering the call to these various ministries prayerfully, there is little power in its work. The prayers of the people during the congregation's worship bear the responsibility of bathing the mission of the church in prayer. Through these prayers, they change what God can do through them as a congregation in ministering to their needs and the needs of the society in which they live.

Korean worship provides a most powerful illustration of the people's work of corporate intercession. As the pastor calls out the various needs for prayer, the people respond not with written words, but with personal words. The sanctuary becomes a great sound of all voices praying in their own way for the need lifted before them by the pastor; the sound of the many voices speaking simultaneously rises in the cadence of prayer. When the voices subside again there is a moment of silence, and then the pastor names the next request. In such a way the whole congregation is filled by the Spirit for the work of intercession. These prayers are released to God one by one, and by the corporate body as a whole, till finally the pastor leads them all in the great Lord's Prayer in thanksgiving.

How we pray the intercessory prayers of the church at worship differs from denomination to denomination and from culture to culture. But through them we are nonetheless united with the church in all times and places, doing the work that is given us to do in prayer, which is at the same time the worship of God. And throughout the world, Christian congregations alike conclude their petitions and intercessions by joining in our unique Christian way of praying, the Lord's Prayer.

Following our intercessions and the Lord's Prayer, we give offerings from our own material resources as an act of worship. We have prayed for the mission of the church, and our first act following these prayers is the prayerful giving in financial support of the church's mission. This most appropriately extends the act of prayer, supplementing our prayers of intercession with gifts for intercession. We support the church as it lives out God's call to address the needs for which we pray.

It is not accidental that our representative offerings to God are often (and in some churches, always) followed by the eucharist, which is God's offering to us. Just as forgiveness is a giving and receiving, and daily bread is a giving and receiving, even so offerings are a great giving and receiving between God and us, and this giving is holy, bathed in prayer. The full liturgy of the service is repeated in miniature around the Supper—there is praise of God, a naming of God's work for us, the petitions of the Lord's Prayer, and the participation in God's great nurturing of us through this physical/spiritual gift of bread and wine: Christ with us.

Finally, the conclusion to our services is a hymn of praise, which repeats the prayer pattern of the early church of beginning and ending with the praise of God. This is followed by the benediction, the "well-saying" that names the grace of God that empowers us as we leave to live our corporate prayers in our personal as well as corporate daily life.

Our communal worship of God is a great praying, uniting us in the name of Christ before God with each other. That such should be given to us to do is itself a matter of great thanksgiving. Whether, like the early

Christians, we come together for this work of worship three times a week, or as is more customary today, once a week, this work of prayer together gives us the rhythm of our lives. Together, we lift our whole selves to God, releasing our whole selves to God. The God who receives us empowers us for the separate and corporate tasks of our weeks and years. At the center of all our tasks is prayer.

I began this chapter by suggesting that the prayers of the church constitute the unity of the church. By participating together in a life of prayer, we participate together in the Christ who prayed for us. We are the extensions of his own praying. Insofar as our prayers are liturgically given in our worship, the very form of the praying whispers its continuity with the prayers of Christians at all times, in all places. Through our praying, we are one with Christ, and one with each other.

CHAPTER NINE

The Lord's Prayer

The oldest Christian liturgical prayer is the Lord's Prayer, for it has been consistently prayed by Christians for the two millennia of Christian history. When we today pray this prayer, in whatever language, we are praying the translated words and spirit of generations of Christians. If God receives us into the divine self and joins us there with our relevant world, are we not then joined with those who have also prayed this prayer? Is there not a deep sense in which we are joined with them in the praise and petitions of this prayer? Since it is the prayer given to us by Jesus, we join in his spirit as we join with each other, offering to God the prayer he taught us.

If we are united with those in our past, it is also the case that we ourselves become the transitional link for those who will follow us. We are the living spirituality of that prayer, and we teach it to the children of the church, raising up yet another generation who will join us in this holy praying. Those who come after us do so through the graced witness of our own generation, constituting the living tradition of Christian prayer. The children of tomorrow are now in our future; we anticipate them in our praying, and thus we are in a sense united with them. In due time, of course, they will take their place as the present generation of the church, and we will be their past. There is a great embracing of the generations in this praying, so that the prayer itself makes us all one.

If the prayer unites us across time, it also unites us across the geographical distances that separate us. I have participated in worship services in countries and cultures not my own; sometimes I have some knowledge of the language, but usually I do not. Yet when the time comes in the service for the people to unite in the cadence of this particular prayer, I know I am at home in the Spirit of Christ. As I softly join in the prayer with my foreigner's tongue, I know that the language of the prayer uniting us is deeper than the differences of speech that otherwise separate us. The Lord's Prayer is itself an ever-living creation of unity akin to the unity manifested in that great high priestly prayer recorded in John 17.

Not only the fact of sharing the Lord's Prayer, but the petitions themselves bring us together. The great prayer begins not with the personal word *My*, but with the common word *Our*. The God we know is mediated by our common tradition, no matter what differences of theology are embraced within it. Because we are Christian, we address God with our shared "our." This is certainly not to deny that peoples of religious faiths other than Christianity address God with their own form of "our," and that they, too, have a distinctive identity that renders their own "our" meaningful to them and to God. But that is God's story with them, not God's story with us. Our story gives us our own common identity around the "our" created through Jesus Christ; we know God in and through Christ, so that we become a distinctive family among the world's peoples—and among God's peoples, too, if in fact God brings all religions into their own unique forms according to the communal richness made possible within their various contexts. We are Christian, and our praying marks us so.

The distinctive naming of God is our "Father," and what difficulties this presents in our current day! We have so overlaid the reality of God with projections of all that we consider best—and sometimes worst—of masculinity that we are close to idolatry, of making God no better than ourselves. We forget the Hosean text that thunders, "I am God, and no man!" And we have made matters worse still by following our projection of masculinity onto God by projecting deity onto men! We have so lifted up the importance of being male that there are still those who claim that women cannot serve God in ordained ministry because and only because women aren't men. What does maleness have to do with serving the God who is beyond gender? How hard it is to redeem Jesus' word for God, "Father," after centuries of our obsession with a presumed higher value for maleness.

Jesus called God "Father" in a century that was even more patriarchal than our own. But his drawing us into that naming, with "*our* Father," is not a vaunting of maleness—for the remarkable nature of Jesus' ministry, and that which set him apart from all other traditions of his time, was his equal value of women and men. His naming of God as "father" in a patriarchal society broke down the privileges that society conferred upon men. Through patriarchy, society was and is ordered according to family lineage, raising some in value and lowering others. In such ordering, one's father determines one's place: The child of the king is given more importance than the child of the outcast. But Jesus gives us all the highest lineage possible when he draws us into the "our" of naming God's own self our "Father." If God is my father and yours, are we not one in value? Is not the social ranking of higher and lower immediately overturned? When Jesus teaches us to join him in calling God "father," with the inclusive pronoun "our," we are invited into a profound sharing with Jesus' own self through the prayer. The "ourness" of the relation to father overturns the patriarchal privilege of "your" father against "mine." In a profound sense, the "our" in the petition radically reverses the societal exclusiveness of "father." When this reversal is recognized, a more authentic naming than father might be "our parent," or "O thou dear creator and gatherer of us all." Such a naming honors the radical message of the "our" that Jesus gives us in the prayer.

Thus in Jesus' prayer the "our Father" breaks the divisive idolatry of projecting maleness onto God, together with the divisiveness of a society that, like ours, too easily knew how to separate persons into the privileged and the debased. By inviting us together to name God as "our Father," Jesus replaced social privilege with the humble privilege of the Spirit. If in our own day the naming of "Father" is no longer capable of carrying this liberating message, then the heart of the prayer is truncated. If we can restore the word to its liberating invitation to sharing as a single family of God, then this aspect of the prayer can be restored to its gospel intent.

The address of "our Father" is followed by a hallowing of the divine name. How is God's name made holy? The next petitions provide an answer: "Thy kingdom come. Thy will be done, on earth as it is in heaven." God's reign comes about as we ourselves are open to that divine guidance offered us in every moment. God's guidance, in turn, leads us toward righteousness, and righteousness is itself the hallowing of God's name. Righteousness on earth mirrors the righteousness of heaven, echoing heaven's holiness, hallowing heaven's name. Insofar as we follow God's guidance, we hallow God's name.

God's guidance always takes account of our context and the larger community. This is necessarily so, because the God who gives guidance to us is also giving guidance to our many neighbors. We live in a world of interdependent well-being. This requires an element of coordination in divine guidance, ideally blending the well-being of each into the well-being of the wider community, and the well-being of that community into the well-being of each of its members. Our own actions toward the good for ourselves must entail as well that which makes for the communal good. It's not that there will never be contradictions between what we see as our good and what we see as the good of the community—far from it. Nor is it that the guidance from God can override the perils of our context. But God's guidance is always toward the best way we can become in these circumstances relative to ourselves and to increasingly wider communities. Our openness to this guidance, so that we become formed by it, is in fact the reign of God in our lives. It leads to lives and acts of caring, of righteousness, of justice.

In a relational universe, this reign of God in our lives becomes an echo of God's will being done in heaven. God receives the world, and transforms it within God's own nature until it is conformed to God; from this divine work, God fashions what reflection of the divine nature the world can bear in its own circumstances. When, then, we integrate God's guidance into who we are, we are to that degree mirroring what God has already done within the divine self. We become in a very particular way an "image of God," responding to God's will on earth as a reflection of God's own heaven.

Again, this reign of God is communal, even while it is personal. God's own self is the immensity of God's relating to the whole universe, with a great will toward its communal well-being. Our minuscule reflection of God's will adapted to us in our time and place will likewise have implications and responsibilities beyond our own small sphere. We must understand ourselves as God's people for the sake of a goodness that is more than our own, a richness that reaches in extensiveness to enhance the well-being of the widest possible world, human and nonhuman.

Insofar as we are open to God's reign, living it in our dailiness, then we are ourselves a hallowing of the divine name. The Jewish prophet Micah put it succinctly: what does the Lord require of you but to do justice, to love mercy, and to walk humbly with your God? Our conformity to this text in all the uniqueness of each of our moments becomes our living prayer in fulfillment of the petition, "hallowed be thy name." By God's grace, we can become participants in that very hallowing for which we pray.

The next petition forms a request for our daily strength and nurturance. We ask for daily bread, representing physical sustenance. But we also ask daily for this bread: the prayer is continuous in intent and effect. It indicates that our sustenance is not self-created and self-sustained, but is in fact dependent on God as well as many others in a relational world. Our sustenance comes to us, and we receive it, through many hands—and in an urbanized society, this is far more profound than in small farming communities. The food on our table comes to us not from the gardens we have tended, but from vineyards in Chile, ranches in Argentina, coffee farms in Costa Rica, rice paddies in Asia, wheat fields in mid-America, and vegetable farms in California. The vast network of the world's food systems transports produce thousands of miles through a chain of industries, quickly making it available to us on our tables.

Give us this day our daily bread! As we lift this prayer for sustenance we cannot do so without gratitude to God's beneficence and the earth's generosity.

To ask daily bread for ourselves is to ask daily bread for all, and to acknowledge our own responsibility in giving as well as receiving sustenance in this great chain. The petition names "us" rather than "me," so that faithful lifting of the prayer involves intercession for all the hungry of this earth. Does bread come to us from those who cannot afford to feed themselves? "Give *us* this day our daily bread," and the prayer calls us to conscience. What is the real price of our daily bread? Do our ways of obtaining sustenance defraud others of theirs? Is there justice in the distribution of food throughout the world? To what extent is it possible for us to participate in the righteousness of God by participating in the feeding of the world's peoples? The prayer for daily bread is a call not only for sustenance, not only for gratitude, but also for responsibility as we take the "us" of the prayer seriously.

Throughout our Christian history we have prayed the petition for daily bread in consciousness of not simply our physical needs, but also our spiritual needs. There have been times in our history when we allowed the spiritual aspect of "bread" to replace the physical aspect, but this does violence to the meaning of the prayer. Nonetheless, since the physical and the spiritual are intertwined, it is right to include the petition for spiritual sustenance in and through our petition for daily bread. The great gift of the eucharist is spiritual bread, given in remembrance of our Lord's last supper. In this supper, bread of earth and bread of heaven become one, and we are fed. We receive through the physical form of bread the tangible witness of God's presence with us and for us in Jesus Christ's life, death, and resurrection. Eating this bread is a participation in the event of Christ, and therefore is a nourishment to our spirits. The two "breads," physical and spiritual, are joined in modest imitation of God's own incarnation in Christ. Even so, we who take this bread together become joined with each other and with the Christ who is given for us. We are united in thanksgiving before God for the great gifts of nourishment of body and soul.

If the petition for bread recognizes our interdependence, the petition for forgiveness does so even more. It assumes that in fact we will need to give and to receive forgiveness, that in our interdependent fragility we will in fact experience violation and inflict violation. The petition does not say, "Forgive us if we trespass," or "Forgive us when we trespass," it simply states the fact: "Forgive us our trespasses as we forgive those who trespass against us." As a daily prayer, it assumes a daily need.

However, the petition for forgiveness is the one petition that attaches a condition to it: we ask God to forgive us as we forgive others. As I noted in the earlier chapters on confession, we are called to be a people who live from the forgiveness of sins, not simply in a passive way, but in an active way. The prayer disallows our grudges; we are to forgive by releasing our ill-being and joining in God's own will toward well-being, even toward those who violate us. For we all have violated God, and God wills us well; the will toward well-being is at the heart of being conformed to God's own image and thus hallowing the divine name.

There is the further implication that as we release ill will toward others we open ourselves for God's own goodwill toward us. Harboring resentment and hatred closes us, causing us to become "stuck" in the event that creates our own ill-being. Releasing this, letting it go, opens us to a new future that begins with our own openness to God. Thus the contingency between our receiving and our giving forgiveness is not arbitrary, but pragmatic. It opens us to conformity with God's own great will toward inclusive well-being in the world.

That asking God for forgiveness does not replace asking others for forgiveness is made quite clear in the full Gospel account, for the petition for forgiveness appears in the same Gospel where we are enjoined, when bringing an offering to the Lord and remembering our sin against another, that we go to that other and ask for forgiveness. Furthermore, that we are called upon to forgive others means that we are also called upon to ask forgiveness of others. And over all is the God who is also violated and who also forgives.

Lead us not into temptation. Has it never seemed strange to you, as it has to me, why such a petition would be included? Would we even think God could or would tempt us in ways that are against our good? The petition seems particularly strange following the petition for forgiveness, and yet this may be the clue to its meaning. Jesus also gave a parable in Matthew 12 in which an "unclean spirit" is cast from a person; the spirit wanders, seeking a resting place, but finds none. Returning then to its original home, it finds the person now well-swept and orderly, but empty. And so the spirit not only takes up residence again, but brings along seven others! Forgiveness of sins is a release from that which hinders us, whether that hindrance be our own violation of others or our own refusal to look to the good of those who have violated us. In a sense, forgiveness "empties" us so that we may then be "filled" with the fruits that follow forgiveness, which are attitudes and actions of goodwill. Can we not understand the petition, "Lead us not into temptation," as a request that we not remain empty, but that our ill will shall be replaced with good? God is the one who faithfully gives us impulses toward our good; we pray that through our receiving and giving of forgiveness, we shall be led not in the same paths of our old sins, but in new paths according to God's good pleasure. Thus "Lead us not into temptation" is paired with "Forgive us our trespasses," and is the logical extension of the forgiveness of sins.

And deliver us from evil. We pray it daily, and too often we—or those we love—do *not* seem to be delivered from evil. There are terminal illnesses, there are dreadful accidents, and there is the particular horror of violence against ourselves and those we love through warfare or terrorism or criminal activity. Deliver us from evil! In our fragility and mortality, there is evil enough. But the prayer seems to recognize this, and its request is not that we shall not experience evil, but that we shall be delivered. In a sense this is to ask that we might live in the resurrection power of God, who is able to work transformation in every evil. There is no evil that God's love for us cannot overcome, for the very nature of God's leading in every moment contains not only the power of endurance, but also the power of transformation. The transformation will be suited to the circumstances.

To me the greatest image of such transformation has always been the recounting of the meeting between Thomas and the resurrected Christ. Thomas had refused to accept the impossible knowledge until and unless he could see for himself that this one who had appeared was in fact the one who had been crucified. The story tells of the appearing Christ with the words, "Put your finger here and see my hands. Reach out your hand and put it in my side." The wounds of crucifixion were not erased, as if the awful death had never occurred; there was no "pretend it didn't happen" associated with that Easter! To the contrary, the very wounds of crucifixion became the sign of resurrection. Even so with us; the evil we encounter is seldom erased from our experience, but we can be transformed from evil's devastation. The shape of our transformation, however, is determined in part by the evil we have encountered. It will be a transformation that could be wrought only in and through whatever form of crucifixion we have experienced.

Undoubtedly, in most if not all ways it would be better if our various crucifixions simply did not occur! Better to be preserved from transformations that come about at so high a price! But we are fragile, and we live in a network that includes violation: We *will* encounter that which threatens to undo us. The petition does not pray that this will not happen, for it would then pray for the impossible. What it does do is draw us into the prayer of trans-formation, of resurrection: deliver us from evil. The very God who delivered Jesus from the evil of the crucifixion by raising him up will also deliver us from the evils we encounter, giving us modes of resurrection that are fitted to our circumstances within our own ongoing stories. God is the one who delivers us from evil.

Jesus ended the prayer with this petition, but the prayer as he gave it was itself an insertion into the larger liturgical prayers of the Jewish community. These prayers began and ended with praise of God. Hence the church now inserts the Lord's Prayer into the larger liturgy of common wor-ship, and also often adds the words, "for thine is the king-dom, and the power, and the glory forever." This conclu-sion owns, as does the beginning, that all our prayers are to God, and that we give ourselves along with our prayers to the divine keeping. Prayer begins and ends with God's own self; prayer is the offering of our own stories into the greater story that is God's drama with the universe, of which we are a part.

CHAPTER TEN

Prayers of Thanksgiving and Praise

I n the deepest sense, all prayers are prayers of thanksgiving and praise. When we confess our sins, whether individually or corporately, we are grateful for the character of God whose very nature is a will toward the wellbeing of all creatures, including us. When we bring prayers of intercession to God, we acknowledge with gratitude God's transformative guidance for us and those for whom we pray. Liturgical prayers likewise express with thanksgiving the unity God provides for the community, which is an echo of the great unity of God. Prayer is thanksgiving, for no matter what specific thing or person may be the subject of our praying, the very fact that we can bring these matters to the one who is God bathes the praying in the overflowing gratitude that is praise.

Yet there are also those prayers that have no other end than giving praise to God, and for these, too, relational theology offers a particular interpretation. Other forms of praying draw particularly on the dynamics that take place between God and the world—that back-and-forth giving and receiving that outlines the dance of the universe. While these are in part prayers of praise, a prayer of pure thanksgiving creates an even more deeply personal dynamic between ourselves and God. These prayers focus not only on the gifts of God, but on the giver of those gifts—on God's own self. Such prayers are often the source of the union we sometimes feel with God. But the order of thanksgiving begins most often with thanks for the specific gifts of God.

It is right to focus on the gifts of God in our prayers of thanksgiving. Indeed, we have example enough of this in the epistles of the New Testament, most of which begin with prayers of thanksgiving to God. In Romans, Paul thanks God for the Romans' witness of faith. In the Corinthian letters, Paul gives thanks for the grace of God given to the Corinthians, and for the spiritual gifts they had received; he also thanks God for God's own leading, and for the spreading knowledge of God. The letter to the Ephesians expresses thanks to God for those receiving this epistle; Philippians begins with the words, "I thank my God every time I remember you," and the letter to the Colossians offers thanksgiving for the faith, love, and hope of those in Colossae. For the Thessalonians, Paul expresses thanks for their works of faith, labors of love, and steadfastness in hope. The letters to Timothy contain thanks for Timothy himself, and also an urging that "supplications, prayers, intercessions, and thanksgivings be made for everyone," particularly rulers. Philemon includes thanks expressed because of Philemon's love and faith.

The rather obvious implication for our own praying is that we are to offer God thanks for communities of faith, and that this thanksgiving especially focuses on the faith, hope, and love that is manifest in and through these communities. It's not that we are to be blind to the communities' faults—indeed, several of the letters that begin with thanks are also quite explicit about failings within the community. But the failings never obliterate the reality that the community is a community of faith, love, and hope, and for this, thanksgiving to God is unfailingly appropriate. Furthermore, it is precisely because the community is fundamentally formed through these gifts of the Spirit that its reform is always possible. Its reformation is always a call to be re-formed according to the attributes of faith, hope, and love expressed within itself and to its wider community. Consequently, no matter what failings may mark the community—and Paul makes it amply clear that the failings can be quite severe—we are to thank God for the community, and for its faith, hope, and love.

Paul's prayers contain a double thanksgiving: thanks for the community itself, and thanks for the community's faith. The implication is that faith, love, and hope are gifts of the Spirit, and therefore God as giver of these gifts is indeed to be thanked. These gifts of God now belong to the community. It's as if God releases the gifts so that the community can make them its own. And of course, taking in these gifts is in fact the very becoming of the community: it is community in and through its owning and living of the gifts of God. There is a double action of gifts given and gifts received, integrated, and therefore actualized as community. Being grateful for the community is also being grateful to the community for its actualization of the divine gifts.

Such an attitude of thanksgiving changes our approach to our community of faith, for it means we can never regard the community apart from the gifts it has received and internalized from God. These gifts are at the very foundation of the community, creating it as community. All conflicts, disagreements, and egregious sins within the congregation are like an overlay that is continuously correctable because of the internalized gifts. One does not abandon the community of faith, or argue for splitting the congregation on the basis of irreconcilable differences. This is because the basis for reform is already within the identity of the congregation. Reform is not to be found by creating a newer, purer group—for all groups, sharing the same gifts of God, are essentially one already. Consequently, the way to respond to the problems within the congregation is to express thanksgiving to God for the community and its faith, love, and hope, even while one attempts to deal in faith, love, and hope with the communal problems. In this case, prayers of thanksgiving for the community and its internalized gifts are simultaneously prayers of gratitude and prayers that themselves are part of the constitution of precisely that community. This is why Paul can write to a congregation such as that at Corinth in genuine thanksgiving, even though his letter is occasioned by the difficult problems that had emerged within the community.

Thanksgiving to God for the gifts of God, then, is to have an "echo effect" in the world: we thank God, and we also thank the ones for whom we are giving thanks. Paul thanks God and the Corinthians. This witnesses to the relational nature of the God to whom we pray, who gives freely to us and to the community, releasing the gifts to us for our own responsive and responsible living. The community or individual could have rejected the gifts of God— in which case it would not now be that community, that individual. So we thank God for giving the gift, and the creature for its own graced response as it makes the gifts its own. The result is that the pervasive act of thanking God

affects our way of living in the world, making us expectant
of seeing God's gifts actualized in those we meet and those
we know. Continuous thanksgiving to God creates a continuous expectancy of encountering gifts God has released
into the world, and that the world has made its own—and
given back to God. God gives gifts to the world; the world
makes these gifts its own by receiving and using them. To
use God's gifts is to give them away, both to the wider
world, and to God's own self. The mystery and the miracle
is that in giving away the gifts God has given us, we are
ourselves immeasurably enriched. God's gifts are for giving, and in the giving, we experience the deepest blessing
of the gift.

Giving God thanks for God's gifts in the world leads
us to thanksgiving not only for communities of faith, but
also for the supportive structure of this earth in all its
wonder and beauty. The Jewish Psalms excel in praising
God for the gift of our environing earth, both by using
nature imagery as an analogy for God, and for direct thanks
for the seasons, the fruitfulness of the earth, and the
flourishing of so many species of life. Indeed, the Psalms
conclude with a marvelous commentary on the creation
text of Genesis 1; they not only portray human thanksgiving to God for God's nature and God's gifts, but they
also portray the entire creation joining the human song
till all the earth swells in a mighty symphony of praise and
thanksgiving to God. The order of creation in Genesis is
matched by the order of praise in the final Psalms.

Our thanksgiving for the earth has a somber note in
these days of realizing that our own power of destruction
can undo creation. Out of ignorance or out of greed, we
have misused the resources of the earth, speeding up the
extinction of some of earth's species and creating conditions
for overpopulation of others, which itself endangers the
ecosystem on which all depend. We have created waste

products that cannot be reabsorbed by the earth, and polluted air, water, land, and forests. We have created instruments for the sole purpose of destruction of each other and the earth that supports us. Therefore, our thanksgiving for the earth needs to be a "walking" prayer so that we ourselves, as individuals and as communities, address the well-being of this earth for which we give God thanks. Confession of contributing to earth's ill-being and intercession for earth's well-being must merge with prayers of thanksgiving for earth's wonder, beauty, and goodness. Our living of such prayers becomes the hope for humanity's conversion from exploitation to conservation and nourishment of the earth that nourishes us.

We give thanks not only for others and for the earth, but also for the faithful guidance of God in our own lives. We become so easily habituated to the faithfulness of God; prayers of thanksgiving "wake us up" to the wonder of God's faithfulness. In every moment of our lives God touches us with an impulse toward our good within the context of our communities, our responsibilities, our past, and our future. This does not mean that we will therefore never encounter any difficulties—far from it! But it does mean that even in those difficulties, God works with us as we are to lead us to where we can be; God is the source of ever-present hope. God's guidance cannot preserve us from all harm; God's guidance can empower us to live lives of faith, hope, and love in and through the harm. God's guiding touch springs from God's own resurrection power, offering us forms of that power fitted to our finite selves. Prayers of thanksgiving acknowledge the continuously giving and receiving God, who wills our well-being in the depths of our living. And so we give prayers of thanks.

I noted earlier that prayers of confession are at the same time reception of God's forgiveness. Such forgiveness is not automatic, even though it stems from the very nature of God. Rather, God's forgiveness is shaped to each person whom God forgives, necessarily so, and this is at great cost even for God. God experiences the world as it is. This means that God receives the world in every moment of its existence, and this reception constitutes God's knowledge of the world. God doesn't know the world because God reads about it in some book, or because God observes it from some safely distant viewing post. To the contrary, God knows the world because God receives the fullness of its energy, in all its particularities, in every moment. When we sin, God experiences the sin. Since the "sinfulness" of sin is its destructiveness of well-being in a violation of love, God's experience of sin is an experience of violation. Nor is it simply that God feels the violation from the perspective of the sinner—not at all, for God feels all the world, and therefore feels all the pain of the ones sinned against. I spoke earlier of the rippling effect of sin. The sinner may know only of the direct results of sin, but God has to experience sin in all of its ramifications in every nook and cranny touched by the destructive ill will of sin. In knowing our world, then, God knows our sin, not abstractly, but experientially. In the fullness of this knowledge, God fashions guidance for our well-being. Confession opens us to receiving this as our forgiveness—but at such a price! The price is God's feeling knowledge of our sin and its effects. Through this knowledge, God's forgiveness is the offer of transformation toward our well-being. The nature of God to receive us, despite the pain of our ill will, and the awesome love of God that wills our good, form the basis for the forgiveness we receive. This knowledge fills us with humility that we have made the price of our forgiveness so dear, and with gratitude that God is just such a God as to forgive us through consistently willing our well-being.

Our Christian witness to this nature of God comes through God's revelation in Jesus Christ. It is for this reason that all the thanks given by the apostle in the epistles are in and through Jesus Christ, for the knowledge of God's acceptance of us and forgiveness of us is mediated to us Christians through Jesus Christ. Our thanks to God are thus shaped by Christ. It is as if Christ is the form, the mold of our thanks. Through the witness of Christ's teachings insofar as they are recorded in the Gospels, we know God to be one who wills good that is inclusive of all, even us; through the witness of Christ's death, we know that God experiences the pain of our sins; through the witness of Christ's resurrection, we know that God is the power of transformation toward the good in every moment of our lives. The knowledge of God mediated to us through Jesus Christ fills us with thanksgiving.

There is a peculiarity introduced into the God-world dynamic when we know that God experiences us as we are. The awful side of this is that God feels the pains we experience and inflict, from every standpoint. But there is another side as well—God also experiences our joys, and the sheer goodness of existence from all of its perspectives. I remember a night during a time of my life when all seemed like despair. My whole world had fallen apart, and the pain seemed almost beyond endurance. The night I remember was during the full moon in midwinter, the ground all covered with snow. Some friends invited me to go coasting on the hills, for the night was bright, despite the lateness of the hour. So we gathered the old sleds, and went through the woods till we came to the hill. Breaking through the woods into the clearing, I suddenly saw the sky filled with subtle changing lights. It was one of those rare occasions when the northern lights could be seen even as far south as Ohio, where I lived at the time. I could not move from the wonder of the scene—so much unexpected beauty! And it seemed to me then that there is a joy of beauty deeper than any pain, and a glory to living and experiencing beauty, no matter what the hardships. And just as my pain and despair had been experienced by God, even so my joy was experienced by God. Sometimes—and I do not think it irreverent to imagine it—it seems to me that in the midst of my joys—whether sharpened by the contrasting pain as on that night, or simply in the goodness of relishing the love of family and friends—I feel a divine whisper of "thanks"—even to me! And I joyously fling back to the God who is always present a happy, "You're welcome!" Isn't it a holy thing, this giving and receiving that takes place between God and the universe, that not only our pains, but our joys are God's as well? We can indeed say "You're welcome!" to God, who also says "You're welcome!" to us. The whole is the fullness of relational thanksgiving.

Our gratitude for the gifts of God leads to gratitude for the knowledge of God, which leads simply to gratitude to God. There is a movement from gratitude for what we have received, to gratitude for what we know, to gratitude that simply loses itself in God. And here is where a further dynamic of the relation between God and the world comes into new focus.

Again and again I have noted that God feels us as we are, and touches us toward our good. That touch from God is always oriented toward us and our condition; it pushes us toward deeper involvement in the world, deeper openness to relation, deeper caring for the well-being of the earth. Thus God's guidance is not like some clarion call to know God; to the contrary, it is an insistent whisper that we shall live responsibly and lovingly in the world. But our thanksgiving to God for God's gift and for God's nature shifts us from our attention to the concerns of the world to God's own self. We move from gift to giver.

God touches us in every moment, and we receive that touch, integrating it into how we are, who we are. But it is a touch from God that we receive, usually unknowingly. We integrate that which is from God into ourselves. In one sense this is simply a way of talking about the constant grace of God and its empowering nature. But if we receive into ourselves that which is from God, then there is something of God's own self that is given with the gift, for all God's gifts are mediated through God's living Spirit. It seems to me that it is possible to follow the gift in the Spirit to the giver, so that the prayers of thanksgiving that we give to God almost take us along with them, till we experience a living sense of God's overwhelming will toward our well-being, which is the love of God. For our own good, I do not think this happens too often or for too long a time. We are not yet fitted to bear too much of God—though in God's own time, we will be so fitted. Until then, we receive these earthly experiences of the glory that is God, and we ponder them in our hearts with great gratitude. Our thanksgiving to God moves from thanks for God's gifts to thanks for God's self; it is as if we touch God back, and experience a sense of God's self as an overwhelming presence of love. Our thanksgiving then becomes swallowed up in joy, which is itself the praise of God.

Prayer is God's great gift that conveys the sense of grace-empowered union between ourselves and God, and between ourselves and one another. It is our avenue of "first resort," not "last resort," in all of life's difficulties. It is the pathway to transformation when we become immobilized through sin, whether our own or another's. It is the cooperative work of continuing creation between God and the world, through which God calls the world toward its further transformation into God's image. Prayer is the life-blood of our Christian living, rhythming our days with faith, hope, and love. In all our praying, then, there is thanksgiving for the gift of prayer itself. Through prayer, we know ourselves as we truly are: in God's presence.

Epilogue

God is like water, flowing throughout the universe, like an ocean touching innumerable shores. The action of those waves is sometimes like a chaotic clash of elements, whose terrible dynamism reshapes what is and brings new things to emergence. And the action of those waves is also gentle and quiet, nourishing all forms of existent life. The one form does not contradict the other, nor the varieties in between, for the nature of water is interaction with all elements in its path, taking the nature of each element into account in the resulting action. God is like water.

And we? Are we those shores touched by God, showing in the shape of our sands what we have done with the waves of God upon our lives? And what of our effects in God as our sands find their way into the vastness of that ocean?

All images break down as we push them to their limits. But the force of this image is to give a sense of the very pervasiveness of God, so that prayer, far from being supernatural or even superstitious, simply follows from the reality that we live in—and within—God's presence.

God creates and works within an interdependent universe, both interdependent within itself and with God. The universe is not "finished"; God's creativity cannot be so easily stilled! Stars are yet born, and race toward unfathomable reaches of space. Suns yet burst in fireballs of energy, spawning yet new planets and who knows what forms of new life. In our own small portion of this universe, generation yet follows generation, and we turn life into story, and yet again into history. In such a teeming universe, what is prayer but God's gracious invitation to us to participate in the continuing work of creation? If prayer constitutes our openness to God's own purposes of increasing communal well-being, then prayer is God's creation *with* us of this very well-being! Prayer is central to the *how* of God's continuing work in our world.

And so our prayers of confession purge us of blockages against our own and others' well-being, opening us to the transforming work and will of God. Prayers of intercession actively join us with God's will toward the well-being of the greater community, and are used by God to whatever degree possible to bring such well-being into existence. Liturgical prayers express and deepen our communal identities, and can open us to goodwill toward communities not our own. We may yet with God turn this world into a community of communities, rejoicing in identities that are what they are in and through their differences as well as similarities! Then we would be woven into a world with a sparkling story, creating together with God a new history of interdependent care for one another and for this wondrous Earth.

And prayers of thanksgiving are like breathing spaces in all the work of prayer and the work that flows from prayer. Gratitude shapes and forms us, flows through us and from us, mingling with our sorrows as well as with our joys. Gratitude is the sheer delight of being a conscious participant in the dance of God, the dance with God.

And now, you see, in the end my image of God as water shifts, becoming the image of the dancing God who woos us to partnership through prayer. But shall we not swim in those waters, dance in that dance, and merge all our metaphors together in gratitude to the One who surpasses them all? Oh yes! So let us pray; so be it; amen.